Criminal Justice
Recent Scholarship

Edited by
Marilyn McShane and Frank P. Williams III

A Series from LFB Scholarly

The Murder of Police Officers

Robert J. Kaminski

LFB Scholarly Publishing LLC
New York 2004

Library of Congress Cataloging-in-Publication Data

Kaminski, Robert J., 1953-
  The murder of police officers / Robert J. Kaminski.
     p. cm. -- (Criminal justice recent scholarship)
  Includes bibliographical references and index.
  ISBN 1-59332-007-8 (alk. paper)
  1. Police murders--Social aspects--United States. 2. Police murders--
Research--Methodology. I. Title. II. Series: Criminal justice (LFB
Scholarly Publishing LLC)
  HV8139K36 2004
  364.152'3--dc22

2004005488

ISBN 1-59332-007-8

Printed on acid-free 250-year-life paper.

Manufactured in the United States of America.

To my parents and Masae and Cody.

Table Of Contents

List of Tables and Figures

Acknowledgements

Completion of this research would not have been possible without the help and support of many people. First and foremost, I thank Dr. David Bayley, Dr. David Duffee, Dr. Colin Loftin, Dr. David McDowall, and Dr. Robert Worden for their support and advice during this endeavor. I also thank Dr. Ronald Everett for reviewing the manuscript and Dr. Akiva Liberman for his programming expertise. Remaining errors and limitations of this work, of course, are entirely my responsibility. Much of this research was completed while I was employed by the National Institute of Justice, and I am indebted to Jeremy Travis, past Director of the Institute, and Dr. Sally Hillsman, past Director of the Office of Research and Evaluation for their understanding and support. Working "two jobs" would not have been possible without it.

Preface

Macro-level research on homicides of police has focused on the influence of structural features of areas that generate criminal motivation. The implicit assumption has been that criminogenic conditions (e.g., high levels of poverty, economic inequality, broken families, population mobility) increase crime, which in turn increases police risk of homicide victimization. With few exceptions, then, theory used to explain spatial or temporal patterns of police homicides have mirrored traditional theories of offender motivation developed to explain crime and victimization generally. Traditional theories of offender motivation, however, ignore routine activities and lifestyles of persons that facilitate or impede opportunities for crime and victimization. Models developed to explain homicides of police also have tended to ignore routine activity factors that likely influence opportunities for the victimization of field officers, particularly organizational differences across police departments or variation in "routine work activities."

This study advances research on violence against the police by incorporating both structural covariates and routine work activity factors in a model of police homicide victimization. Based on criminal opportunity theory, it is hypothesized that differences in levels of exposure to motivated offenders and officer physical and social guardianship across 190 municipal law enforcement agencies in four time periods influence opportunities for murders of police, once the effects of criminogenic structural conditions of the jurisdictions in which agencies are located have been taken into account (i.e., proximity to motivated offenders). Given the generally inconsistent results obtained in previous research, particular attention is paid to statistical modeling issues, such as collinearity among regressors, clustering, and the rare-event count nature of the dependent variable.

Multiple regression analyses reveal that measures of social (e.g., proportion of one- vs. two-officer patrol units) and physical guardianship (e.g., mandatory vest-wear policies) are unrelated to homicides of police at the macro level. Rather, homicides of police are primarily a function of exposure (arrests) and proximity to motivated offenders (criminogenic structural conditions). That the indicators of guardianship are proxy measures that may suffer from substantial measurement error, however, precludes definitive conclusions regarding their lack of effects. Further research on the influence of social and physical guardianship using improved measures is warranted. Additional research is also needed to determine why agencies located in the South and those employing more females experience greater numbers of police homicides.

Introduction

It has long been recognized that the risk of police homicide victimization[1] varies across jurisdictions (Brearley, 1934), and contemporary researchers have attempted to identify the correlates of police homicides at various levels of areal aggregation. Macro-level analyses have been conducted at the level of *nations* (Kaminski and Marvell, 2002; Peterson and Bailey, 1994; Southwick, 1998); *states* (Bailey, 1982; Bailey and Peterson, 1987; Chamlin, 1989; Peterson and Bailey, 1988 *counties* (Kaminski, Jefferis, and Chanhatasilpa, 2001), and *cities* (Fridell and Pate, 1995; Jacobs and Carmichael, 2002; Lott, 2000). Although laudable, the results have not been very informative because research findings have been inconsistent (see, e.g., the summary in Kaminski and Marvell, 2002). To gain a more thorough understanding of the relationship between homicides of police and social, demographic, and economic conditions, continued research on the macro-structural correlates of police homicides is necessary.

The emphasis of the prior research on structural covariates, however, implies that the determinants of police homicide risk are for the most part a function of conditions external to potential victims. In other words, risk largely is deemed to be a function of adverse social and economic conditions of the jurisdictions in which law enforcement agencies operate. Consequently, little consideration has been given to how variation in organizational arrangements across law enforcement agencies influences opportunities for homicides of police officers. Because this is a relatively unexplored area of research, it is unknown whether differences in homicide risk across geographical areas are due, in part, to differences in agency-level organizational structures or whether the differences are solely or primarily a function of community characteristics that are largely beyond the control of local police departments.

Since little is known about the determinants of risk, the goal of this study is to advance research by examining the relative impacts of organizational- and community-level factors on police homicide risk. This is important because the findings may have implications for theory and practice. If it is found that cross-agency differences in the structure or organization of police work influences the risk of homicide net of community correlates, than integrating these factors into explanatory models may advance theory. If community-level factors are paramount, it may be beyond the ability of police departments to reduce by any substantial degree officer risk of homicide victimization. Broad reductions in crime and violence likely would be required to decrease substantially murders of officers and there would be few implications for police policy and practice. If, however, findings show that differences in the organization of police work influence homicide risk once criminogenic structural conditions are controlled for, they would have important implications for police policy and practice related to officer safety.

The organization of the book is as follows; Chapter 1 introduces criminal opportunity theory and its relevance for studying lethal assaults on police. Major concepts of the theory are described and the empirical and theoretical support for indicators of the concepts used in the study is presented. Formal hypotheses appear at the end of this chapter. Chapter 2 presents a brief historical overview of research on homicides of police, followed by detailed reviews of the 10 previous multivariate studies of macro-level correlates of police homicides. Chapter 3 discusses the sources of data and various issues pertaining to the dependent and independent variables. This discussion is followed by the operationalization of variables. Chapter 4 presents the methods used and the results of the analysis. This includes descriptive statistics, bivariate analyses, estimation of cross-section Poisson regression models, and estimation of a panel model using generalized estimating equations. Chapter 6 provides a discussion of results and conclusions.

CHAPTER 1

Criminal Opportunity Theory and the Murder of Police

CRIMINAL OPPORTUNITY THEORY

The importance of opportunity structures for explaining patterns of crime and delinquency was implicitly recognized early in the twentieth century by such noted criminologists as Burgess (1916), Thrasher (1963), and Shaw and McKay (1969), and later in the work of Cloward and Ohlin (1960). Early victimization studies also highlighted the role of victims in creating opportunities for crime (Hans von Hentig, 1948; Wolfgang, 1958). However, it was not until the works of Hindelang, Gottfredson and Garofalo (1978) and Cohen and Felson (1979) that theory regarding the influence of opportunity structures on rates of crime and victimization was more fully developed (Miethe and Meier, 1994:2-3). Although Cohen and Felson (1979) developed *routine activity theory* to explain changes in crime rates over time, and Hindelang, Gottfredson, and Garofalo (1978) developed the *lifestyle-exposure model* to explain differences in victimization risk across social groups, both theories emphasize how "patterns of routine activities or lifestyles in conventional society provide an opportunity structure for crime," with the differences between them being primarily a matter of terminology (Garofalo, 1987:27; Maxfield, 1987:276; Miethe and Meier, 1994:470).

Hindelang, Gottfredson, and Garofalo (1978:241) define lifestyle as "routine daily activities, both vocational activities (work, school, keeping house, etc.) and leisure activities." Variation in lifestyles across groups leads to differential exposure to lower or higher risk locations, times, and persons, and hence, different levels of victimization, with differences in lifestyles being determined by role expectations and structural constraints (e.g., economic, familial, educational). Demographic characteristics such as age, sex, race, and income are indicators of the structural constraints and role expectations that shape lifestyle, but are not part of the causal sequence in the lifestyle-exposure model (Garofalo, 1987:26).

According to Cohen and Felson (1979:589), direct-contact predatory crime rates (e.g., robbery, assault) are influenced by structural changes in routine activity patterns that affect the convergence of motivated offenders, suitable targets, and the absence of capable guardians in time and space. They define routine activities as "any recurrent and prevalent activities that provide for basic population and individual needs" (p. 593). This includes formalized work, leisure, and the pursuit of other basic human needs and desires such as sexual expression and companionship.

A variety of social changes can lead to increases (or decreases) in criminal opportunities, e.g., changes in family living arrangements (more single person households), self-protective measures taken by the public, and decreases in the size and weight of manufactured products (e.g., televisions, VCRs). Importantly, the theory allows consideration of the relative contributions of the proportion of motivated offenders and the proportion of suitable targets in explaining crime rate trends. Cohen and Felson (1979:589), for example, argue that "if the proportion of motivated offenders or even suitable targets were to remain stable in a community, changes in routine activities could nonetheless alter the likelihood of their convergence in space and time, thereby creating more opportunities for crimes to occur."

RELEVANCE TO OCCUPATIONS

Although routine activity theory and the lifestyle-exposure model recognize how changes in the structure of the work force affects criminal opportunities and victimization rates (e.g., increases in female exposure to motivated offenders; reductions in home guardianship), neither theory explicitly addresses the relationship between type of occupation and the probability of victimization. However, substituting the words *employee* and *occupation* for *person* and *lifestyle*, respectively, in Hindelang, Gottfredson, and Garofalo's (1978:251, 253) first two propositions indicates the potential applicability of the theory to occupations:

Proposition 1: The probability of suffering a personal victimization is directly related to the amount of time that a person [employee] spends in public places (e.g., on the street, in parks, etc.), and particularly in public places at night.

Proposition 2: The probability of being in public places, particularly at night, varies as a function of lifestyle [occupation].

Restated, Proposition 1 suggests that persons whose jobs more often involve exposure to public places increases victimization risk. Taxicab drivers and law enforcement officers' jobs both involve extensive contact with the public, often at high-risk times and in high-risk places, and both occupations suffer the highest on-the-job homicide rates (Jenkins, 1996:7). Cab drivers typically are robbery victims, whereas police officers typically are killed by offenders engaged in serious crime who wish to avoid apprehension and punishment (Cardarelli, 1968; Creamer and Robin 1970; Margarita, 1980b). Cab drivers and police officers, therefore, experience high rates of victimization not as a function of lifestyle, but as a function of their occupation. Jobs that require high levels of face-to-face interaction with the public is a risk factor (Collins, Cox, and Langan, 1987; Lynch, 1987).

Hindelang, Gottfredson, and Garofalo (1978:270) recognized the potential applicability of their theory to workplace victimization. Under suggestions for future research they state:

> In this chapter we referred generally to persons employed outside the home, in contrast to homemakers, unemployed persons, retired persons, and so forth. But there are certainly variations within these categories—for example, related to type of occupation—that have major ramifications for lifestyle. For example, do those whose occupations involve work in public places have higher rates of personal victimization than those who work in private places?

Researchers subsequently examined the effects of occupation-related exposure and attractiveness on risk of violent victimization on the job, and they recognized that police face special job-related risks (see, e.g., Block, Felson, and Block 1984; Collins, Cox and Langan,,

1987; Lynch, 1987). But empirical studies have not tested whether variation in the major components of opportunity theory (proximity and exposure to motivated offenders, guardianship, and attractiveness) *within* the occupation of policing affects officer risk of victimization.

Thus, the model of police officer victimization developed here is not concerned with variation in opportunity structures and risk *across* occupations, or inter-occupational variation in victimization risk. Rather, the interest is in the development of a model of intra-occupational variation in risk of victimization, i.e., whether variation in the structure of work across police agencies differentially impacts officer risk of homicide victimization. The model, therefore, largely has an organizational focus: it is not the lifestyles/routine activities of individuals or social groups that are examined, but differences in departmental policies, practices and work patterns that may influence officer vulnerability, exposure, attractiveness, and proximity to motivated offenders.

COMBINING STRUCTURAL AND OPPORTUNITY FACTORS

Although development of the lifestyle and routine activity theories was viewed as a major advance in criminology, one limitation of traditional opportunity models is that structural conditions that generate criminal motivations or free individuals to engage in crime, such as poverty, population heterogeneity, and residential mobility, are downplayed, largely neglected, or assumed to be constant (Maxfield, 1987:276; Miethe and McDowall, 1993:743; Miethe and Meier, 1994:34; Miethe, Stafford, and Long, 1987:193).

As stated by Miethe and McDowall, (1993:743), "Opportunity theories of victimization . . . place importance on the routine activities and life-styles of persons that enhance their accessibility and attractiveness as targets for victimization, but these theories generally ignore the social forces that produce criminal motivations." Conversely, traditional theories of offender motivation ignore how variation in routine activities and lifestyles facilitate or impede opportunities for crime (Miethe and Meier, 1994:xii). Thus, the development of explanations of crime and victimization that consider both structural and opportunity factors seems a logical direction for research on predatory crime, and there is substantial empirical support for models that integrate these two perspectives (Miethe and McDowall, 1993:745).

The major research question to be addressed in this study, then, is whether variation in the structure or organization of police work impacts opportunities for the victimization of officers, once effects of social, demographic, and economic conditions are controlled. By explicitly taking into account the supply of motivated offenders, the supply of suitable targets (police), and factors affecting their convergence in time and place, the model should be better able to explain the geographic distribution of police homicides than previously has been the case. To summarize, the risk of police officer homicide victimization is viewed, in part, as a function of variation in the policies, practices, and deployment patterns of police forces that structure opportunities for contact between motivated offenders and officers.

Next, the major concepts of criminal opportunity theory are explained. The variables used as indicators of the concepts and their relevance for explaining cross-agency variation in police homicide risk are also discussed. Specific hypotheses and operationalization of variables are presented later.

EXPOSURE

Exposure is defined as "variations in physical visibility and accessibility of potential targets (persons or objects) to potential offenders as determined by personal characteristics of the potential targets" (Cohen, Kluegel, and Land, 1981:507, note 3). The assumption here is that more frequent physical contact between motivated offenders and potential victims increases opportunities for offenders to victimize potential targets. All else equal, then, it is expected that an increase in visibility and accessibility of potential victims to potential offenders leads to an increase in victimization risk (Cohen, Kluegel, and Land, 1981:508; Miethe and Meier, 1994:39).

As an example for violent crime, Miethe and McDowall (1993:749) use public activity in dangerous places (e.g., bars, nightclubs, public transit) as a measure of exposure. Thus, given some level of physical proximity to motivated offenders (e.g., because of residential or job location), one's activity in the proximate environment constitutes exposure.

Similarly, given deployment of police in the field (conceptualized in this study as a component of proximity), there are a number of factors that likely affect officer visibility and accessibility to motivated offenders (exposure). At the organizational level, for instance, an administrator's decision to reassign some officers from a low crime area to a high crime area within a jurisdiction would increase their exposure to motivated offenders, as would a decision to reassign desk officers to the field. At the individual level, variation in officers' propensity for maintaining order and enforcing the law would differentially expose them to suspects and offenders.

Variables used as indicators of exposure in the analysis are limited by data availability, but an expected important indicator is arrests made by police. Another is the proportion of field officers assigned to foot vs. motorized patrol. A third candidate, although conceptualized primarily as a measure of guardianship, is discussed briefly in this section because it is arguably related to both exposure and guardianship. This is the proportion of officers assigned to one-versus two-officer patrol units.

Arrests

From an opportunity perspective, arrests made by police is a close parallel to the exposure-related concept of *non-household* activities (leisure, employment) used in routine activity/lifestyle approaches to crime (Miethe and Meier, 1994:48). Arrests have been used in research as an indicator of the aggressiveness or activity level of police departments, and variation in arrest activity is thought to be related to officer risk of assault (Chamlin and Cochran, 1994; Handberg, Unkovic, and Feuerstein, 1986).

In his study of the of varieties of patrol officer behavior, Wilson (1975) observed substantial differences across agencies in the way police performed their functions, particularly in the decision to make arrests for less serious offenses. Although not specifically concerned with how variation in patterns of arrest activity across agencies impacts the risk of officer victimization, Wilson (1975:19-20) did recognize a link between levels of enforcement and order maintenance activities and officer exposure to physical danger.

In Wilson's watchman-style departments, patrol officers are encouraged to ignore the "little stuff" with informal settlements being the rule for minor offenses (Ibid., 145-146). Legalistic departments encourage officers "to handle commonplace situations as if they were matters of law enforcement rather than order maintenance" and to intervene formally rather than informally by making arrests. Thus, for example, officers will "make large numbers of misdemeanor arrests even when . . . the public order has not been breached" (Ibid., 172-173). Service style agencies where "police intervene frequently but not formally" fall between watchman and legalistic agencies (Ibid., 200).

Borrowing from Wilson (1975), Handberg, Unkovic, and Feuerstein (1986:2-3) argue that aggressive police agencies engage in patrol patterns that are more proactive, and thus "create additional situations of heightened exposure to violence", while "[m]ore passive departments (in Wilson's typology, the 'watchman style') reduce their exposure because many criminal activities never come to their attention in any form or are effectively ignored by the department if it is made aware of the activity." Though it is not stated, service style agencies presumably fall somewhere in the middle regarding exposure to violence.

In studies of violence against the police, therefore, it may be important to distinguish between aggressive or legalistic police agencies, i.e., those agencies where officers are encouraged to maximize the number of interventions and enforce the law, and more "passive" agencies (watchman and service), where officers may less frequently stop suspicious persons or motor vehicles and more often respond to discretionary situations informally (Wilson and Boland, 1978). It is important to do so because, assuming approximately equal levels of crime, patrol officers employed by legalistic agencies will tend to experience more contacts with suspects and criminals and make more arrests than officers employed by watchman- or service-style agencies. Higher levels of contact with suspects and criminals and greater numbers of arrests are assumed to increase opportunities for officer victimization, other factors being equal.[2]

Wilson (1975) and Wilson and Boland (1978) used traffic enforcement as a proxy measure of departmental "aggressiveness", but Wilson and Boland (1978:371) recognized that "police in some cities may be aggressive about enforcing the traffic laws but lax about making street stops, checking suspicious persons, or employing other specialized patrol techniques." Given the questionable utility of traffic stops as an overall proxy for an aggressive patrol strategy, plus the fact that traffic citation data are not available in the Uniform Crime Reports (UCR), an alternative measure is needed.

Wilson (1975:86,145) suggested that arrests for other less serious offenses, such as gambling, vice, public intoxication and disorderly conduct, might serve as adequate proxies. Crank (1990) used arrest rates for four non-Index offense categories for his measure of agency aggressiveness (minor vandalism, disorderly conduct, motor vehicle offenses and a drug-related offense). Langworthy (1988:7) proposed using the residuals from a regression of a city's arrest rate on its crime rate as an alternative measure of police aggressiveness, because "communities that have higher arrest rates than would be predicted from crime rates are exhibiting more aggressive arrest behavior than other cities."

Unfortunately, a problem with this proposed measure is that the number of offenses known to the police is available only for Part I crimes—not Part II crimes, which is the preferred proxy measure of aggressiveness (Wilson, 1975). Langworthy (1988:7-8, note 3) suggests therefore, a

> measure [that] includes all arrests in the regression on index offenses... [T]he index offense rate is presumed an indicator of opportunity to arrest rather than the manifestation of the opportunity to arrest... The presumption is that opportunities to arrest for non-index offenses is positively related to the index offense...rate and that it is therefore appropriate to regress all arrests on the index offense arrest rate. This measure taps more arrest variation than the index offense arrest based regression because it includes the more discretionary less serious offenses.

However, two arguments can be made against this approach. One is that Part II crimes suffer from greater measurement error (reporting and recording biases) than Part I crimes (Schneider and Wiersema, 1990). A second is that most homicides of police are committed by criminals perpetrating serious crimes (Cardarelli, 1968; Creamer and Robin 1970 ; Margarita, 1980b). Offenders committing minor crimes are unlikely to be motivated to murder police as their "opportunity costs" are expected to be lower (assuming, e.g., they are not already wanted for a previous serious crime). Said another way, it is not expected that many contacts between police and suspects engaged in minor criminal behavior would escalate into deadly force situations, whereas one *would* expect proportionately more deadly-force situations to arise out of contacts between police and offenders engaged in serious criminal activities.

This is not to say that aggressive enforcement of minor offenses does not result in suspect resistance and minor assaults on police, nor the occasional fatal assault on an officer. However, offenders committing serious crimes can be expected, on average, to offer greater levels of resistance because their opportunity costs are much higher (e.g., longer prison sentences). Thus, it should take fewer contacts between police and offenders engaged in serious crime to generate one fatal attack on an officer.

Given the above discussion, is seems most appropriate to use arrests for serious offenses as a measure of officer exposure to motivated offenders. While this measure is not an indicator of agency aggressiveness as originally conceived by Wilson (1975), it does mitigate the problems of measurement error associated with less serious crime statistics (Schneider and Wiersema, 1990).

Empirical Findings Regarding Arrests

Indicators of police aggressiveness or activity levels in studies of homicides of police have been limited to arrests for Index offenses (Chamlin, 1989; Fridell and Pate, 1995). Chamlin (1989) used the aggregate Index crime arrest rate per 100,000 sworn officers, but it was statistically insignificant in all models estimated. Fridell and Pate (1995) used the number of violent and property crime arrests per 100,000 sworn officers. Neither measure was statistically significant in their 1985-1992 model. In their 1977-1984 model, the violent crime arrest rate was inversely related to police homicides, whereas the property crime arrest rate was positively related. Although not examined in many studies, arrests for Part I offenses as a predictor of homicides of police is not well supported.

Foot Versus Motorized Patrol

In a study of work-related victimization, Lynch (1987) measured exposure using the number of job-related face-to-face interactions persons had within a given period of time. A direct measure of the number of face-to-face interactions police have with the public is unavailable for the departments included in this study,[3] but the percentage of police assigned to foot patrol may increase aggregate levels of officer visibility and accessibility. Although there appear to be no theoretical discussions in the policing literature about the level of officer exposure as a function of assignment to foot versus motorized patrol, Langworthy and Travis (1997:368) observe that with the widespread adoption of the patrol car "[p]olice officers were removed from the face-to-face contact with citizens they had enjoyed when patrolling on foot," and Peak (1997:154) notes that the renewed interest in foot patrol in the 1960s in 1970s was in part a response to the view that officers should be less isolated from the public and leave their "mechanized fortresses" to walk the beat. Thus, if officers on foot patrol experience more contacts with the public than officers on motorized patrol, they may also experience more conflict that increases their risk of victimization (Blau and Blau, 1982:119; Chamlin, 1989:358; Kieselhorst, 1974:58).

Note, however, as the discussion regarding arrests indicated, the risk of homicide is expected to be much higher for police confronting offenders engaged in serious criminal activity. Therefore, although higher percentages of officers assigned to foot patrol across agencies may be associated with more face-to-face contacts with the public, the conflicts and assaults arising out these contacts are undoubtedly most often minor and nonfatal. The proportion of police assigned to foot patrol, therefore, may be only weakly related to police homicide victimization.

A further limitation of the foot patrol measure is that it ignores potential variability in activity levels and assignment differentials of foot officers and officers in vehicles. Officers assigned to motorized patrol, for instance, may be dispatched to many more calls for service than foot patrol units, what is frequently referred to as "chasing the radio." Motorized patrols also may be dispatched to different—and perhaps more dangerous—situations than officers on foot patrol, and their contacts with the public may generally be less confrontational than officers on vehicle patrol (Trojanowicz, 1982). Although this study is unable to distinguish among these possibilities, the net effect of patrol assignment will be captured by including an indicator of the proportion of the force assigned to foot patrol.

Empirical Findings Regarding Foot Patrol

The only empirical research on the risk associated with assignment to foot patrol versus motorized patrol is purely descriptive in nature.

Typical of such analyses, Little (1984:72) and Fridell and Pate (1995:70) tabulated national data on the number and percentages of officers killed feloniously in the line of duty assigned to each type of patrol. Although these studies show that relatively few foot patrol officers are murdered, an accurate assessment of the risk of homicide associated with type of patrol assignment cannot be made without an appropriate denominator or base rate (Garner and Clemmer, 1986; Sherman, 1980b).

One- Versus Two-Officer Units

Patrol unit size is used in this study primarily as an indicator of guardianship (discussed in detail later), but it is important to mention here that variation across police departments in the proportion of officers assigned to one- versus two-officer units impacts the level of patrol unit density, and thus affects officer exposure as well. Although additional factors are likely to be relevant (e.g., the relative degree of vulnerability and variation in activity levels associated with one- versus two-officer units), it seems reasonable to expect that given two police departments with equal numbers of patrol officers, the agency that assigns a greater proportion of its field officers to one-officer units will increase officer visibility and accessibility. Unfortunately, it is not possible to differentiate among the possible relationships in this study, as increases in the proportion of one-officer units is likely to simultaneously impact officer vulnerability and exposure. In other words, if a positive association were observed between the proportion of one-officer units and homicide, it would not be possible to know whether it was due to increased exposure, increased vulnerability, or both.

GUARDIANSHIP

Cohen, Kluegel, and Land (1981:508) define guardianship as "the effectiveness of persons...or objects in preventing violations from occurring, either by their presence alone or by some sort of direct or indirect action." The assumption is that, all else equal, offenders prefer unguarded or less well-guarded targets over well-guarded targets because the latter increase the "costs" to likely offenders, i.e., well-guarded targets require greater effort and increase the risk of detection and apprehension (Miethe and Meier, 1995:51).

As indicated by Cohen, Kluegel, and Land (1981), guardianship consists of both physical and social dimensions. Social guardians typically are "ordinary citizens going about their daily routines whose mere presence serves as a gentle reminder that someone is looking" (Felson, 1998:53). Their presence alone may prevent crime, or they may prevent crime by offering assistance in repelling an attack (Miethe and Meier, 1994:51).

Physical guardianship consists of various target-hardening activities (e.g., locks on windows, burglar alarms, guard dogs, firearm ownership), other physical impediments to household theft (e.g., street lighting, guarded entryways), and collective actions such as neighborhood watch programs (Miethe and Meier, 1995:51). Physical guardianship may also consist of characteristics of persons that make them appear more capable of successful defense against an attack. As Cook (1986:9) points out, "[p]otential targets that appear capable and willing to defend themselves will be less victimization prone than others." Similarly, Felson (1998:54) argues that if potential victims are "too bulky or strong for potential offenders to overcome, a violent crime probably will not occur. Violent offenders usually pick human targets who are weak, outnumbering them with co-offenders…and making sure that capable guardians are absent." Miethe, Stafford, and Long (1987:193) note that some persons or groups, e.g., males, young persons, though perhaps more visible and accessible may be less suitable as targets because of their presumed greater physical ability to resist an attack and "serve as their own guardians", what might be called *self-guardianship*.

Because police are repeatedly exposed to potentially violent persons and situations, law enforcement agencies, to varying degrees, take steps to reduce officer vulnerability. These include the adoption or modification of policies, strategies, tactics, and technologies designed to reduce officer risk of attack, injury, and death. Examples are mandating that all line officers wear bulletproof vests when on duty, providing officers with improved firearms and new less-lethal weapons, having officers patrol in pairs, and training in conflict resolution skills and defensive tactics. As will be shown later, there is substantial variation in these factors both across and within agencies over time.

Given opportunity theory arguments regarding guardianship, it is reasonable to hypothesize that some potential assailants choose not to assault police who, say, are better armed, wear body armor, and are in the presence of other officers. Further, better-trained police may choose approaches, strategies or tactics that lessen their risk of victimization, or they may be more effective in the application of physical force once resisted or attacked (e.g., hand cuffing, self defense, handgun retention, shooting accuracy). Available data allow the consideration of several such factors. These are patrol-unit size, mandatory vest-wear policies, types of authorized weapons (semiautomatics vs. revolvers; pepper spray), and training requirements.

Patrol Unit Size

Issues of cost, efficiency, and officer safety have been the core concerns regarding the relative merits of one- versus two-officer patrol units (Boydstun, Sherry, and Moelter, 1977), but there has been little theoretical discussion or empirical tests of an association between varieties of patrol unit staffing and risk of officer victimization. Opponents of two-officer patrols argue that paired officers are more likely to be distracted during patrol and tend to be overconfident in hazardous situations, which presumably increases officer victimization risk. Advocates of two-officer patrols, however, claim they provide "built-in" cover for an arresting officer and increase officer acuteness of observation (Boydstun, Sherry, and Moelter, 1977:7-8; Wilson, Brunk, and Myer, 1990:270).

Thus, the idea that two-officer units provide greater protection for police than single-officer units is compatible with the notion of "social guardianship" in opportunity theory (Felson, 1998:53-54; Miethe and Meier, 1995:51), and it may be that potential police assailants are more reluctant to initiate an attack against paired officers than lone officers (Wilson, Brunk, and Myer, 1990:270). Further, when assaults on police occur, having two officers present rather than one may increase the odds of successfully subduing assailants before officers are seriously injured. When a paired officer does sustain a life-threatening injury, his or her partner may be able to provide immediate first aid, summon help, and/or promptly transport the wounded officer to a medical facility, thereby reducing the chances of a serious injury becoming fatal.

Empirical Findings Regarding Patrol-Unit Size

Patrol unit size has not been examined in the macro-level research on homicides of police. Simple tabular analyses, though, show a greater percentage of lone officers murdered than officers in two-person units (Fridell and Pate, 1995:70; Little, 1984:72). Fridell and Pate speculate that "solo patrols without the possibility of quick backup might be a contributing factor" to the relatively high incidence of murders of lone officers (*One-officer state police*, 1997:14). However, the higher incidence of murders of lone officers is probably due to one-officer patrol units being much more common than two-officer units (see, e.g., the variable UNIT1 in Table 5.2). Therefore, an accurate assessment of the risk associated with assignment to one- versus two-officer units requires baseline information on the total number of officers assigned to each, not just the assignments of those murdered (Garner and Clemmer, 1986; Sherman, 1980:8b).

Although not examining homicides of police, two studies found reductions in the probability of injury among assaulted officers assigned to two-officer patrol units (Ellis, Choi, and Blaus, 1993; Wilson, Brunk, and Myer, 1990). Another study, however, found no difference in the likelihood of assault or injury among one- and two-officer units (Boydstun, Sherry, and Moelter, 1977). Kaminski and Sorensen (1995) found that lone officers were *less* likely to be injured when attacked as compared to when two or more officers were attacked. Wilson, Brunk, and Meyer (1990) also found that the number of officers present during assaults incidents was positively associated with officer injury.

While the latter two studies suggest that lone officers are less likely to be injured when assaulted than are accompanied officers—perhaps because unaccompanied officers confronting suspects and criminals are more cautious—the association may be spurious because other officers may respond or be dispatched to particularly volatile situations (Kaminski and Sorensen, 1995). Thus, these findings cannot be used to counter the argument that the presence of a partner fails to increase social guardianship during homicide attempts.

Bulletproof Vests

Analyses of police homicide trends show a relatively constant and steep decline since 1973 in the number and rate that has continued well into the 1990s (Kaminski and Marvell, 2002; Quinet, Bordua, and Lassiter, 1997). That this decline occurred as police employment and violent crime levels rose suggests the influence of some protective factor(s). Several explanations have been proposed, such as the use of body armor and improvements in training, tactics, and emergency medicine (Fridell and Pate, 1995; Kaminski and Marvell, 2002; Quinet, Bordua, and Lassiter, 1997).

The adoption of body armor by police may have been the greatest contributor to the decline. For instance, using a case-control design, the FBI estimates the odds of dying are 14 times greater for officers not wearing vests (*Law enforcement officers killed and assaulted*, 1994:7), and Knight and Brierley (1998:23) report that during 1987-1997 some 1,247 assaulted officers survived potentially fatal injuries because of body armor. Further, police began to adopt body armor around 1973 (Estey, 1997), which is coterminous with the beginning of the decline in police homicides.

Although there is little doubt that body armor protects officers struck in the vest by a caliber of bullet for which the armor was designed to stop, there are no accurate data on body armor wear rates that can be used to estimate their impact on police fatalities (Brown and Langan, 2001:20). Data on agency mandatory vest-wear policies, though, are available, and it is reasonable to expect that vest wear rates are higher in these agencies than in those where the decision to wear body armor is left to officer discretion (Geller and Scott, 1992:133). If mandatory vest-wear policies are effective in increasing wear rates, then they should reduce the probability of fatal shootings.

Officers may be further protected because some potential assailants may be deterred from shooting police they believe are wearing body armor (e.g., greater likelihood of capture and punishment if the officer survives being shot; fear of being shot in return fire). A reasonable hypothesis, then, is that of an inverse relationship between mandatory vest wear policies and homicides of police.[4]

Empirical Findings Regarding Bulletproof Vests

Studies attempting to estimate the impact of body armor on officer mortality are limited by a lack of data on actual vest use (Brown and Langan, 2001:20). Kaminski and Marvell (2002) tested two proxy measures of vest usage. One was the percentage of police killed feloniously while wearing vests. Another was a variable coded zero to

1972 and a linear trend thereafter, because the first "save" by vests was reported in 1973 (Estey, 1997). Conducting a multivariate time series analysis, these authors found no evidence of a protective effect using these measures. Lott (2000:258), using year, city, and county fixed effects, found no relationship between police homicides and mandatory vest-wear policies. In contrast to these findings, however, an unpublished study by Kaminski (1998) found mandatory vest-wear policies to be *positively* associated with homicides of municipal police in cross-sectional Poisson regressions, probably because departments in high-risk cities are more likely to implement such policies.

Police Training

There is little theoretical discussion in the policing literature regarding the salience of training for reducing officer victimization. Kieselhorst (1974:60-61), however, argues that training to improve police performance will not significantly reduce attacks on police. Other researchers, though, argue in favor of improved training for reducing murders of police. For instance, in-depth studies of incidents in which 106 law enforcement officers were murdered or nearly murdered in the line of duty found that victim officers often made tactical errors, such as improper approaches and failure to conduct thorough searches ([Pinizzotto and Davis], 1992; Pinizzotto and Davis, 1997).

> Confirming what has long been the opinion in the law enforcement community, routine, repetitive tasks emerged as a continuing threat to officer safety. Traffic stops, communicating with the dispatcher, communicating with other involved jurisdictions, searches, use of handcuffs, etc., are examples of tasks that should be second nature to officers but posed problems to the victims in the cases studied. (Pinizzotto and Davis, 1997:4)

Officers that survived their attacks frequently cited repeated safety training as being critical to their survival, whereas other victim officers cited "inadequate or improper training that actually made them unsure of the proper action" (Ibid., 4). Analysis by the authors of the circumstances surrounding the incidents in which officers were murdered indicated a number of areas in which training may be deficient, including approaches to vehicles and suspects, control of persons, facing a drawn gun, weapon retention, searches, handcuffing, and night training (Ibid., 36).

Other researchers speculate that that improvements in police training contributed to the observed decline in the rate of officers killed feloniously in the line of duty over the last two decades (Fridell and Pate, 1995; Quinet, Bordua, and Lassiter, 1997), and Chapman (1998:77) states that "training is the single most important factor in preventing an officer from becoming a statistic [and that] it is undertraining that has led to the victimization of officers."

Scharf and Binder (1983:165) suggest that high levels of skill with unarmed tactics and a variety of less-than-lethal weapons can, under some circumstances, reduce the likelihood of potentially violent or violent encounters from escalating into armed confrontations, thereby avoiding the use of deadly force. They write, for instance:

> Often, physical skills are important. An officer who can physically control an opponent, may in some circumstances, avoid a level of threat that would warrant the use of deadly force. Speed in apprehending a suspect, in cuffing him, and in getting him into the police car may thus avoid some escalated armed confrontations. (p. 161)

Although they are suggesting highly skilled officers are less likely to need to resort to the use of deadly force, logic implies that highly skilled officers may gain control of some violent and potentially violent offenders early on during encounters, before the offenders can effectively martial attacks that result in serious or fatal injuries to officers.

To the extent that such skills are a function of the type, frequency, or duration of particular kinds of academy and in-service training (e.g., conflict resolution, mediation skills, "verbal judo", armed and unarmed defensive tactics, cuffing techniques), training for violence reduction and officer survival is compatible with the concept of physical or self-guardianship (Felson, 1998:54; Miethe and Meier, 1995:51).

Unfortunately, there is little information available regarding the types or amount of time police training academies and police departments devote to specific sets of skills. A 1990 survey of the 72 largest American municipal and county police departments did find substantial variation in the amount of defensive tactics training provided to recruits and officers. Specifically, the percentage of time devoted to academy self-defense instruction ranged from a low of two percent to a high of 20 percent, while actual hours of instruction ranged from a low of 10 to a high of 148 hours (Strawbridge and Strawbridge, 1990). Variation at the extremes may affect officers' ability to gain control of resistive and combative suspects and defend themselves from attack. If so, officers with little training may be less able to prevent situations from escalating into armed confrontations, and therefore may be at greater risk of being seriously injured and killed (Scharf and Binder, 1983:161).

For the agencies included in the present study, information only on the total hours of academy training is available. However, to the degree that total training time is correlated with the amount of time devoted to instruction in mediation skills, defensive tactics, shooting skills, etc., the total amount of academy and in-service training time may serve as a rough proxy for the amount of time devoted to instruction in officer safety and survival skills. The assumption, then, is that the greater the amount of total training received, the better police are at handling conflict and protecting themselves.

Empirical Findings Regarding Police Training

There appears to be no empirical research on the relationship of the amount of academy training and homicides of police, but a study by Kaminski and Martin (2000:140-141) suggests that additional training in defensive tactics may increase officers' abilities to defend themselves from attack and subdue resistive and/or combative suspects.

Chemical Agents

Arming officers with effective, less-than-lethal (LTL) weapons for incapacitating resistive and assaultive suspects is compatible with the concept of physical guardianship in opportunity theory (Miethe and Meier, 1995:51) and the notion that violent offenders tend not to choose targets perceived as being less vulnerable (Felson, 1998:54). Officers armed with electrical stun devices, chemical agents, or other LTL weapons may therefore be less susceptible to attack in the first place, and the use of LTL weapons may end some violent encounters early on, before they escalate to armed confrontations. "Skills with a nightstick, sap, flashlight, chemical shield, or mace can avoid some uses of deadly force. And various new nonlethal weapons show promise of ending a confrontation without a shooting" (Scharf and Binder, 1983:165).

Although the most widely issued LTL weapon for law enforcement officers is the police baton or one of its variants (Kaminski, Edwards, and Johnson, 1998:3), batons are rarely utilized by police during use-of-force encounters (Bayley and Garofalo, 1989:21; Garner, Buchanan, Schade, and Hepburn, 1996:5; Fridell and Pate , 1995:74), and therefore are unlikely to be associated with preventing violence against police during regular patrol. The next most widely issued LTL weapon is oleoresin capsicum or "pepper spray" (Kaminski, Edwards, and Johnson, 1998:3). Oleoresin capsicum is a naturally occurring chemical derived from hot peppers that acts as an inflammatory agent by causing swelling of the eyes and breathing passages. Considered to be much more effective at incapacitating resistive and combative subjects than it predecessor "mace" (CS/CN), oleoresin capsicum is carried in small canisters by line officers in most major police departments (Ibid., 3).

There are several reasons why oleoresin capsicum is likely to reduce attacks on police. First, personal-issue pepper spray canisters are small, light, and carried on officers' utility belts, thus making them available for use during most potentially violent encounters. Second, pepper spray is typically authorized for use on the low ends of police use-of-force continua, and thus is applicable for use in a wide variety of resistive and forceful encounters. Third, research suggests it is highly effective against resistive and combative suspects about 70 percent of the time, and that it is moderately effective about 85 percent of the time (Ibid.). Thus, police use of chemical agents may be particularly effective at preventing some forceful encounters from escalating into deadly force situations (Scharf and Binder, 1983:161), thereby reducing the risk of injury and death to some officers.

Empirical Findings Regarding Chemical Agents

Although there is no research on the availability of pepper spray and homicides of police, there is some empirical support for the notion that it deters assaults on police. An interrupted time series analysis conducted by Kaminski, Edwards, and Johnson (1998), for example, found that the introduction of oleoresin capsicum into the Baltimore County Police Department significantly reduced the number of assaults on officers. Other research also suggests that pepper spray reduces the incidence of use of force between officers and suspects, officer and suspect injuries, and excessive force complaints (Gauvin, 1994; *Pepper spray evaluation*, 1995, Lumb and Friday, 1997; Morabito and Doerner, 1997). Because the authorization of chemical agents may reduce attacks on police, it seems reasonable to test the hypothesis that it may also prevent some fatal assaults.

Semiautomatic Handguns

In considering the role of police handguns in influencing police homicide risk over time, Southwick (1998:595) wrote:

> It might be argued that US police are safer than civilians because they are armed with handguns on a regular basis and can better deal with threats to their safety. This argument might be persuasive if police were formerly less likely to be armed and have become more likely to be armed. Then, their risk would be declining. However, police have generally carried handguns for many years in the US, so there has not been a change in this factor.

What Southwick does not account for is that there have been substantial changes in the types of handguns carried by American police. The Colt or Smith & Wesson .38 Special revolvers were standard issue during the 1960s and 1970s, but in the 1980s police began to adopt high-capacity 9mms, in part because of reports of the poor performance of the .38 Special in shootouts with well-armed offenders (Mulroy and Santiago, 2000). The presumed protective benefits of semiautomatic pistols is that they usually have larger ammunition capacities and permit a more rapid rate of fire, and thus have the potential for increasing the number of persons hit and wounds inflicted per shooting incident (Koper and Reedy, 2001). The size of the ammunition for 9mms has also increased up to 147 grains (Mulroy and Santiago, 2000), potentially providing police with greater "stopping power."

Thus, the replacement of revolvers with semiautomatic pistols may provide a tactical advantage to police, particularly as they increasingly face offenders armed with semiautomatic and fully automatic weapons (Geller and Scott, 1992:345). Not only may officers be more likely to survive shootouts when armed with semiautomatic weapons, some potential assailants may be deterred from attacking when cognizant that officers in a particular jurisdiction are carrying semiautomatics.

Empirical Findings Regarding Semiautomatic Handguns

There appears to be no empirical research on the relationship of type of firearm carried by police and homicides of police.

ATTRACTIVENESS

Attractiveness is a third major component of opportunity theory, and is typically conceptualized as the symbolic or economic value of targets to offenders (Garofalo, 1987:38-39; Miethe, Hughes, and McDowall, 1991:166; Miethe and McDowall, 1993:749). Cohen, Kluegel, and Land (1981:508) differentiate target attractiveness as to whether the "motivation to take action against a specific person or object is primarily *instrumental* (i.e., the act is a means of acquiring something one desires) or *expressive* (i.e., the act of attacking a person or stealing is the only reward sought in doing so)" (emphasis in original). Regarding "assault and most criminal homicides, the payoff is not financial but rather, typically, the assailants' satisfaction in hurting those who have threatened, insulted, or otherwise angered them" (Cook, 1986:9).

The concept of attractiveness as applied to the victimization of police officers requires substantial redefinition. Some police may be murdered by mentally ill assailants or because of their "symbolic" value (e.g., perceived as representatives of a repressive government), but because most officers are murdered by offenders engaged in serious crime who wish to escape and avoid punishment (Cardarelli, 1968; Creamer and Robin 1970; Margarita, 1980b), instrumental rather than expressive motives can be attributed to most offenders' decisions to kill police. The motivation is not to harm police because they are despised or because officers do something to anger offenders. Rather, most offenders are motivated to kill or seriously injure police because the potential opportunity costs associated with their current and/or past criminal activities are high (e.g., safety, loss of freedom, reduced future income). Further, most active criminals wish to avoid police, and are unlikely to seek officers out as "attractive" targets. Thus, the target selection process as usually conceived in opportunity theory, except in rare cases, does not apply to an opportunity model of police homicides.

If it is assumed that most offenders murder police because they wish to avoid punishment, it is also reasonable to assume that offenders' motivation to murder varies by the seriousness of their criminal history and the current offense. Bank robbers should be more inclined than shoplifters to seriously injure or kill police confronting them; a car thief with a long and serious criminal history should be more inclined to seriously injure or kill a pursuing officer than a car thief who is a first-time offender. Therefore, police working in areas or jurisdictions with greater proportions of offenders (and/or more active offenders) committing serious crimes should be subject to increased risk of assault and homicide, other factors being equal.

This argument assumes that costs to criminals are similar for the offense being committed and that same offense plus murder. However, almost all suspected police murders are apprehended—98.9% for the years 1986-1995 (Pinizzotto and Davis, 1997:4, 37), and state laws specify police murder as grounds for the death penalty or include it as an aggregating factor (Palmer, 1998:28 and Table A-6). Consequently, it may be argued that criminals are largely deterred from killing police who are attempting to arrest them because the costs associated with killing them are too high. Although there is no research on the deterrent effects of the certainty of punishment on police homicides, there is no evidence that more severe penalties (the death penalty) deter offenders from murdering police (Bailey, 1982; Bailey and Peterson, 1987; Bailey and Peterson, 1994; Kaminski and Marvell, 2002). Thus, the hypothesis that police in jurisdictions with greater numbers of offenders engaged in serious criminal activity are at greater risk of being murdered than are police in jurisdictions with fewer such offenders seems plausible.

Possible useful measures of "attractiveness" (or perhaps more accurately, offender motivation), is the number of Part I crimes known and criminogenic conditions. The assumption here is that the greater the level of known serious crime and/or the more severe the criminogenic conditions in an area, the larger the pool of motivated offenders (and/or more active offenders) committing serious crime. Since in these areas offender opportunity costs are expected to be higher than in areas with little serious crime and/or less severe criminogenic conditions, it is anticipated that, on average, offenders in high crime areas are more likely to forcefully resist, assault, and kill police when threatened with arrest, other factors being equal.

Said a different way, in areas where most crime is trivial, one would not expect most offenders threatened by arrest to find arresting officers highly attractive "targets" for murder, as the average offender is unlikely to be highly motivated to murder or seriously injure police to avoid rather minor punishment. In areas where much crime is serious, the attractiveness of police as targets for murder should be greater because of greater threats to offenders' freedom and safety. Thus, cities with higher levels of serious crime and/or higher levels of poverty, heterogeneity, family disruption, population mobility, and so on are expected to produce more assaults, injuries, and homicides of police.

Unfortunately, although criminogenic conditions and crime levels of areas may in part reflect the attractiveness of police as targets, these factors also are indicators of the concept of proximity to motivated offenders (see below). Thus, there is no independent measure of attractiveness in the analysis, and it is necessarily assumed that more severe criminogenic conditions and/or high levels of serious reported crime increase both spatial proximity to motivated offenders and the attractiveness of police as targets for homicide.

Furthermore, attractiveness is also, in part, a function of "the perceived inertia of a target against illegal treatment," and "the physical capacity of persons to resist attack" (Cohen, Kluegel, and Land, 1981:508). Therefore the concept of target attractiveness also overlaps with the concept of guardianship, and one may assume that police in agencies who are less well protected (e.g., no mandatory vest-wear policy; single-officer patrols) are more attractive to offenders as potential victims.

PROXIMITY

A final major assumption of criminal opportunity theory is that the closer the geographical proximity of potential targets to motivated offenders, the greater the risk of victimization (Sampson and Wooldredge, 1987:372). Cohen, Kluegel, and Land (1981:507) define proximity as "the physical distance between areas where potential targets of crime reside and areas where relatively large populations of potential offenders are found." Proximity clearly is a *spatial* concept: "Being in spatial proximity to motivated offenders tends to increase the frequency of regular contact of offenders with potential victims and thus increases the opportunity for offenders to act against a potential victim and/or his/her property" (Ibid., 508).

Cohen et al. (1981:507, note 3) explain that proximity differs from exposure in that proximity "is a physical relational property pertaining to physical distances between residential locations of populations of potential targets and potential offenders," whereas exposure "pertains to variations in physical visibility and accessibility of potential targets (persons or objects) to potential offenders as determined by personal characteristics of the potential targets." They further note that of "two potential targets whose personal characteristics imply equal exposure (e.g., household structure, employment status), but who differ in proximity, the person in closer proximity to populations of potential offenders will have a higher risk of victimization" (Ibid., 507-508).

It is desirable to develop a spatial measure of proximity based on specific information about the geographical deployment of police relative to geographical location of motivated offenders within areas of a city for the present study. Unfortunately, this is not possible. Point or address data on offenders' residences, locations of criminal events, and information about the geographic deployment of police units within jurisdictions are not routinely available for many large cities. Even if the data were available, homicides of police are too infrequent for multivariate analyses below the agency/city level (e.g., block group, census tract). Because of lack of requisite data for calculating spatial distances between motivated offenders and potential victims, the association between proximity as originally defined by Cohen, Kluegel, and Land (1981:507) and police homicide risk is not able to be assessed.

Given the difficulties of obtaining spatial measures, proximity to motivated offenders is typically measured using indicators of criminogenic conditions of areas, such as population mobility, ethnic heterogeneity, and economic strain (see e.g., Hough, 1987:361-362; Miethe and Meier, 1994:47; Sampson and Wooldredge, 1987:378,387-388). Miethe and McDowall (1993:747-748) explain that from a social disorganization perspective criminogenic conditions in areas increase motivations toward crime, while from an opportunity perspective they "increase victimization risks by increasing individuals' exposure to motivated offenders, target attractiveness, and reducing the level of social control or guardianship." In other words, criminogenic forces "generate a facilitating context for crime by increasing the pool of potential offenders. The greater one's proximity to these criminogenic areas, the greater one's risk of victimization" (Miethe and Meier, 1994:44).

Common indicators of criminogenic conditions (or pools of motivated offenders) are measures of economic strain (e.g., poverty, income inequality, unemployment) and community control (e.g., population mobility, racial heterogeneity, family disruption). Note, however, that Miethe and Meier (1994:47) suggest that the "average rate of offending in an individual's immediate neighborhood is probably the best single indicator of proximity." Therefore, both measures of criminogenic conditions and reported levels of crime are considered in the analysis.

Economic Conditions

Four economic variables are used in the analysis as indicators of criminogenic conditions. These are poverty, income, income inequality, and unemployment. Absolute deprivation or poverty is typically defined as income below that required to maintain a healthy standard of living (Balkwell, 1990:53; Parker and McCall, 1997:36). Poverty and low income have been linked to higher rates of crime because conditions that encourage criminal behavior (e.g., need for income, leisure time) are more pronounced in such areas and because social control mechanisms are weaker (Brantingham and Brantingham, 1984; Bursik and Grasmick, 1993; Krivo and Peterson, 1996; Sampson, Morenoff, and Earls, 1999; Sampson and Raudenbush, 1999).

Relative deprivation, typically measured using the Gini index or some other measure of income dispersion (Balkwell, 1990:53) represents "the presence of blocked and unrewarding legitimate means, whereby the blocked means are perceived as unjust and thus generate resentment" (Parker and McCall, 1997:37). The sense of social injustice and frustration is thought to lead to increased potential for aggression and violence (Balkwell, 1990; Blau and Blau, 1982; Blau and Golden, 1986; Messner, 1982). Unemployment is also thought to represent blocked opportunities that generate frustrations leading to diffuse hostility and aggression (Parker and McCall, 1999; South and Cohen, 1985:326).

Empirical Findings Regarding Economic Conditions

Empirical results regarding the relationship between civilian homicides and poverty and measures of economic inequality have largely been supportive (Land, McCall, and Cohen, 1990; Parker, McCall, and Land, 1999). Results regarding unemployment and civilian homicides have been more mixed, however. South and Cohen (1985), for example, found that the *level* of unemployment was significantly and inversely associated with homicide rates, while *changes* (increases) in unemployment rates were significantly and positively associated with homicides. This supports their notion that unemployment can have both positive and negative impacts, i.e., that it increases motivations for crime while simultaneously decreasing opportunities for crime. A major review of related studies by Chiricos (1987), though, found most support for a positive relationship between unemployment and crime, including homicide. More recent reviews of the empirical literature on the correlates of homicide most often found statistically null associations with unemployment, and where statistically significant relationships were observed, the direction usually was inverse (Land, McCall, and Cohen, 1990; Parker, McCall, and Land, 1999).

Several studies of homicides of police included as indicators of economic strain poverty, income inequality, unemployment, (low) income, the consumer price index, and inflation (Jacobs and Carmichael, 2002; Kaminski and Marvell, 2002; Peterson and Bailey, 1988; Peterson and Bailey, 1994). Chamlin (1989:357), arguing instead a conflict perspective, used both poverty and income inequality as measures of the "presence of threatening groups." Jacobs and Carmichael (2002) share a similar perspective. Operationally, however, these measures are the same as those used in studies that do not embrace a conflict perspective. Other studies also included economic variables in their regression models, but the theoretical rationale for their use was not explicated (Bailey, 1982; Bailey and Peterson, 1987, 1994; Fridell and Pate, 1995).

Chamlin (1989) found significant and positive relationships between poverty and homicides of police in 2 of 3 models estimated, and Bailey and Peterson (1987) found significant and positive relationships in 6 of 12 regression models estimated. Bailey (1982) and Peterson and Bailey (1988), however, found significant and positive relationships in only 2 of 11 and 2 of 8 regression models, respectively. Jacobs and Carmichael (2002) found no significant relationship between poverty and murders of police. Though the poverty-police homicide relationship is one of the most consistent found in the prior literature, overall the evidence for an association is not very strong.

Only three studies of police homicides included measures of income inequality, with mixed results overall. Peterson and Bailey (1988) included measures of income inequality and racial income inequality, but no significant effects were observed for either variable. In the study by Chamlin (1989), income inequality was significant in only one of three models estimated, and the direction of the effect was opposite that anticipated. Jacobs and Carmichael (2002) included two related measures; these are the Gini index of income inequality and the ratio of black to white median household income. These authors found no significant effect for the Gini index, but they found consistent support for the ratio median household income measure, showing that cities with larger racial income differences experienced more homicides of police.

Of the five studies that included unemployment (Bailey, 1982; Jacobs and Carmichael, 2002; Kaminski and Marvell, 2002; Lott, 2000; Peterson and Bailey, 1994), only one (Bailey, 1982) found it to be associated with police homicides (positively), but it was statistically significant in only 3 of 11 regression models estimated. (Lott does not report effects for unemployment.) The empirical evidence for a relationship between homicides of police and unemployment, therefore, is very weak.

Three studies included income, with mixed results (Fridell and Pate, 1995; Kaminski and Marvell, 2002; Lott, 2000). One found support for a significant and inverse relationship between income and police homicides (Kaminski and Marvell, 2002), whereas another found no significant effect (Fridell and Pate, 1995). (The study by Lott does not report estimates.)

Economic measures less commonly used were either unrelated to homicides of police or the findings were mixed (see Table 2.1). These regressors are consumer prices and inflation (Kaminski and Marvell, 2002), welfare (Peterson and Bailey, 1994), and a three-item index comprised of the percentage of families below the poverty level, the Gini index of income inequality, and percent African-American (Fridell and Pate, 1995).

Social Control

Residential mobility, racial heterogeneity, racial segregation, family disintegration, and large and dense populations are structural features of communities thought to be associated with weak formal and informal social controls, and thus with higher levels of crime and delinquency (Bursik and Grasmick, 1993; Kornhauser, 1978; Krivo and Peterson, 1996; Sampson, Morenoff and Earls, 1999; Sampson and Raudenbush, 1999; Shaw and McKay, 1969).

Residential instability is a key theoretical construct of social-disorganization theory (Shaw and McKay, 1969), which argues that high levels of population mobility disrupt a community's social relations and control, leading to higher rates of offending (Kornhauser, 1978; Sampson and Groves, 1989).

High levels of racial/ethnic heterogeneity also impede communication, patterns of interaction, and the ability of residents to achieve consensus and control, thus increasing the potential for crime and delinquency (Parker, McCall, and Land, 1999; Sampson and Groves, 1989; Shaw and McKay, 1969).[5] However, most studies of homicide have simply used percentage black population as a measure of racial heterogeneity (Land, McCall, and Cohen, 1990; Parker, McCall, and Land, 1999), and therefore do not capture the full range of racial and ethnic variation in communities (see, e.g., Sampson and Groves, 1989:784-785).

Nevertheless, the percentage of the population that is black is preferred in the present study because rates of violent crime tend to be especially high in poor, black urban communities (Blau and Blau, 1982:115; Parker, 2001:89; Wilson, 1987:22), and because African Americans represent about 12 percent of the population, but comprise 43 percent of the felons who murder police (Brown and Langan, 2001). Therefore the relative size of this population across cities is expected to be associated with levels of serious violence against the police.

In addition to the racial composition of areas, several civilian homicide researchers have examined the effects of racial *segregation* (Land, McCall, and Cohen, 1990; Parker, McCall, and Land, 1999). As found by Massey (1990:329), residential segregation plays a crucial role in the concentration of urban poverty and the creation of a spatially isolated black underclass. Other social and economic disadvantages are linked to segregation as well, such as high infant mortality rates, unemployment, low levels of education, and violence (Krivo and

Peterson, 1996:621; Shihadeh and Maume, 1997:256; Sorensen, Taeuber, and Hollingsworth, 1975:126). One explanation for high levels of violence in racially segregated areas is that segregation is an ascriptive and structured form of inequality that generates frustration and hostility (Blau and Blau, 1982:119). Cities with large segregated black populations, therefore, may be linked not only to higher levels of violence generally, but higher levels of violence against the police as well.

Consistent with social disorganization theory (Shaw and McKay, 1969), family disintegration (percentage of children living in single-parent households, percentage divorced) has been linked to decreases in informal social controls as single-parent households decrease supervision and guardianship for their own children and household property, as well as general activities in the community (Sampson, 1985; Sampson and Groves, 1989). It is assumed, therefore, that as community levels of family disruption increase, crime and delinquency increase, which in turn increase opportunities for contact between motivated offenders and police.

Large and dense populations are thought to increase crime and delinquency because they weaken interpersonal ties and inhibit social participation in local affairs, leading to a breakdown in social control mechanisms (Brantinham and Brantingham, 1984:151-155; Land, McCall, and Cohen, 1990:927; Sampson, 1986:5; Sampson and Groves, 1989:781-782). Increases in population size and density are also thought to increase the likelihood of social contact and interpersonal conflict (Blau and Blau, 1982:119; Blau and Golden, 1986:16), proximity to motivated offenders (Cohen, Kluegel, and Land, 1981:508), and opportunities for the commission of predatory crimes (Felson, 1998:29-33). Large and dense populations, therefore, are also expected to increase opportunities for contact between police and motivated offenders and the victimization of officers, other factors being equal.

Empirical Findings Regarding Social Control

Prior research on homicides of police has not examined the impact of residential mobility, but there is some evidence it is associated with civilian homicides and other crime (see, e.g., Land, McCall, and Cohen, 1990; Parker, McCall, and Land, 1999; Sampson, 1985; Sampson and Groves, 1989; Sampson and Wilson, 1995).

Eight studies examined the relationship between racial/ethnic composition of areas and homicides of police, using percent black, Hispanic, or minority as measures. Three studies found no statistically significant relationships (Fridell and Pate, 1995; Peterson and Bailey, 1988; Peterson and Bailey, 1994). Four others found only weak support for an association; Bailey (1982) found that percentage nonwhite was significant and positive in only 2 of 11 regression models. Bailey and Peterson (1987) found percentage black to be significant in only 2 of 12 models, and the direction of the effect was positive in one model and negative in the other. Chamlin (1989) examined both percentage black and percentage Hispanic, and found the former significant and positive in 1 of 3 models and the latter significant and positive in 3 of 6 models estimated. In their monthly time series analysis, Peterson and Bailey (1994) found the percentage black inversely related to homicides. Jacobs and Carmichael (2002) found significant and positive relationships between percentage black and murders of police in only two of ten regression models, but they found significant and positive relationships between killings of police and growth in the percentage of the black population in eight out of eight models. Lott (2000) included race in his study, but estimates were not provided. Although findings regarding race · and police homicides generally are weak and inconsistent, most studies on civilian homicides find significant, positive relationships with the percentage of the population that is black (Land, McCall, and Cohen, 1990; Parker, McCall, and Land, 1999).

A number of studies have linked levels of racial segregation to civilian homicides and other forms of violence, but the results have been mixed (Land, McCall, and Cohen, 1990; Parker, 2001; Parker, McCall, and Land, 1999). Only one prior study examined the effect of racial segregation on murders of police. Jacobs and Carmichael (2002) found consistent support for a relationship, but interestingly officers were significantly less likely to be killed in cities with *higher* levels of black racial segregation. The authors argue this is likely due to greater precautionary measures taken by officers patrolling cities with a large spatially isolated black underclass (Ibid: 1243).

A substantial number of studies examining the relationship of civilian homicides to family structure (e.g., percent divorced; percentage of children living in single-parent households) found significant effects in the expected direction (Land, McCall, and Cohen, 1990; Parker, McCall, and Land, 1999). Studies by Chamlin (1989) and Peterson and Bailey (1988) found divorce significantly and positively associated with homicides of police in 3 of 6, and 2 of 8 models, respectively. In a time series analysis, Bailey and Peterson (1994) also found a positive and significant relationship, as did Kaminski and Marvell (2002) in one of two regression models. Jacobs and Carmichael (2002) found consistent support for this variable in the expected direction, but not for the percentage of female-headed households, the only previous study to examine this factor.

Research on the association between population density and civilian homicides has produced mixed results, showing no relationship, a positive relationship, or an inverse relationship (Land, McCall, and Cohen, 1990; Parker, McCall, and Land, 1999). Research by Land, McCall, and Cohen (1990), however, found a consistent and positive association between population *structure* (a combined measure of population size and density) and homicides across time (1960, 1970, and 1980) and unit of analysis (city, SMSA, state).

Research by Fridell and Pate (1995) on the relationship of population density to murders of police produced mixed results (it was not statistically significant in their 1977-1984 model, and although statistically significant in their 1985-1992 model, it was inversely related to police homicides). Jacobs and Carmichael (2002:1247, note 11) also examined population density, but found it was unrelated to murders of police.

Although studies of civilian homicides often find significant and positive effects of population size (Land, McCall, and Cohen, 1990; Parker, McCall, and Land, 1999), except for the study by Lott (2000), population size has rarely been examined in the police homicide literature. Jacobs and Carmichael (2002) consistently find statistically significant positive effects of population size on homicides of police, but a significant quadratic term indicates the effect diminishes after a certain population threshold is reached. Lott (2000) included population size as a control, but does not report estimates and tests of statistical significance for this variable.

Offenses Known To The Police

As discussed earlier, an alternative to using criminogenic conditions of areas as measures of proximity to motivated offenders is the reported level of offending in an area (Miethe and Meier; 1994:47), the assumption being that higher levels of crime in areas increase opportunities for the victimization of police (Chamlin, 1989:358; Peterson and Bailey, 1988:228).

Empirical Findings Regarding Offenses Known To The Police

Five studies of homicides of police include measures of known Index offenses. Overall, however, the empirical evidence for a relationship is weak. Chamlin (1989) found a significant effect in three of six regression models, but the direction of the effect was opposite that hypothesized. Bailey and Peterson (1987) and Peterson and Bailey (1988) found no significant effects. Fridell and Pate (1995) found positive and significant effects for violent crime (two of two regression models) and property crime (one of two regression models). Jacobs and Carmichael (2002) also find consistent, positive effects between murders of police and the violent crime rate (nine of nine models). They also found homicides of police were related to the civilian murder rate, but not the robbery rate (tested simultaneously in one model only).

Field Officer Density

As previously discussed, an assumption of opportunity theory is that the probability of victimization is, in part, a function of the spatial proximity of potential victims to motivated offenders (Cohen, Kluegel, and Land, 1981; Sampson and Wooldredge, 1987). Ideally, then, one would want measures of the spatial location of potential targets relative to the spatial location of potential offenders. In this study, however, the best measure of the location of potential victims is the total number of police officers assigned to field duties within a jurisdiction. It is assumed, therefore, that increases in field officer density increases their spatial proximity to motivated offenders, and therefore opportunities for contact and conflict (Blau and Blau, 1982:119; Chamlin, 1989:358; Kieselhorst, 1974:58). In other words, it is expected that the physical distance between motivated offenders (indicated by criminogenic conditions and/or crime) and field officers (potential victims) decreases with increases in the density of field officers, offenders, or both, and that the likelihood of officer victimization is greatest in cities with the highest levels of police officer and offender density.[6]

Empirical Findings Regarding Field Officer Density

Among the prior studies of homicides of police, only Chamlin (1989) included a measure of police strength on the right-hand side of the regression equation (the number of full-time sworn law enforcement officers per 1,000 population). This variable, however, was significant in only two of six models, and was inversely related.

ADDITIONAL REGRESSORS

To reduce the chance of specification error, several additional variables will be included in the analysis as controls. Structural controls are unit location in the South, population age structure, and population gender stratification. Additional policing-related controls are police agency gender stratification and agency educational requirements for recruits. The latter two regressors have been little studied or have not been included in prior research, and theory regarding them is not well developed.

The South

Unit location in the South has been included in several previous studies of police homicide victimization, but often with little or no theoretical explication (Bailey and Peterson, 1987:11; Chamlin, 1988; Jacobs and Carmichael, 2002; Peterson and Bailey, 1988:218; Fridell and Pate, 1995; but see Kaminski, Jefferis, and Chanhatasilpa, 2000). However, substantial theoretical and empirical work has focused on cultural/subcultural differences for explaining violent behavior among a variety of groups, including southerners (Corzine, Huff-Corzine, and Whitt, 1999; Newman, 1979).

Cultural/subcultural explanations for the observed high levels of homicide in the South essentially posit that the southern subculture provides greater normative support for violence in upholding values such as honor, courage and manliness, though not necessarily a culture that condones violence (Corzine, Huff-Corzine, and Whitt, 1999, Gastil, 1971; Hackney, 1969). Cultures more supportive of expressions of physical aggression and combat in response to threats to one's honor or as a measure of daring and courage increase the likelihood of violence and homicide (Wolfgang and Ferracuti (1982:215). Other research, however, questions the southern culture-homicide argument, suggesting instead that structural poverty and economic inequality accounts for the higher levels of homicide observed in the South (Blau and Blau, 1982; Loftin and Hill, 1974; Smith and Parker, 1980; Williams, 1984). Regardless of the causes, it is expected that risk is greater in the South.

Empirical Findings Regarding Unit Location In The South

Most studies examining the relationship between civilian homicide rates and unit location in the South find either significant effects in the expected direction or null effects (Land, McCall, and Cohen, 1990; Parker, McCall, and Land, 1999). Regarding homicides of police, simple tabular analyses have shown that the South does experience a greater-than-expected number of police killings, even when controlling for regional variation in levels of violent crime, arrests, population size, and number of officers employed (Cardarelli, 1968; [Pinizzotto and Davis], 1992; 1997; Fridell and Pate, 1997; Geller and Scott, 1992). Further, a county-level spatial analysis by Kaminski, Jefferis, and Chanhatasilpa (2000), although controlling only for population size, indicates that police homicides cluster significantly in the southern region. However, they also found that accidental police deaths clustered similarly, suggesting that factors other than a violent subculture may account for the clustering of police homicides in the South.

Only four multiple regression studies of police homicides included an indicator of the southern region. Three found no association (Jacobs and Carmichael, 2002; Peterson and Bailey, 1988; Fridell and Pate, 1995), and a third found a significant effect in only two of twelve models estimated (Bailey and Peterson, 1987), providing little evidence of a relationship.

Sex Stratification

It is well established that the relative proportion of males to females in the population is associated with higher crime rates, particularly serious criminal behavior and homicide (Brantingham and Brantingham, 1984). A number of explanations for sex differences in offending and victimization have been offered, including explanations rooted in psychology, biology, culture, social structure, and opportunity structures (Miethe and Meier, 1994:34; Messner and Rosenfeld, 1999:32-34; Wilson and Hernstein, 1985:115-125). A full review of these explanations is beyond the scope of this study, suffice to say that a higher proportion of males in a population is expected to correlate with higher levels of crime and violence, and thus increased opportunities for violence directed against the police.

Empirical Findings Regarding Sex Stratification

Of the prior studies on killings of police, only Bailey and Peterson (1987) included the population sex ratio as a correlate. The sex ratio was statistically significant in five of twelve estimated regression models, but the direction of the effect was mixed. Some studies of civilian homicides found statistically significant relationships in the expected direction, but many studies also found null relationships (Land, McCall, and Cohen, 1990; Parker, McCall, and Land, 1999).

Age Structure

Although the implications of the age-crime relationship for research continues to be a matter of debate among criminologists, there is a long-standing observation in the criminological literature of the propensity of young adults and teenagers to commit more crime than persons at other ages (Hirschi and Gottfredson, 1983; Land, McCall, and Cohen; 1990). Thus, higher proportions of teenagers and young adults in cities are expected to be associated with higher levels of crime (Messner and Rosenfeld, 1999:36) and opportunities for victimization of police.

Empirical Findings Regarding Age Structure

Some studies examining the relationship between civilian homicides and the proportion of teenagers and young adults show a positive relationship, but most often the associations are null (Land, McCall, and Cohen, 1990; Parker, McCall, and Land, 1999). However, in their reanalysis of the correlates of homicide across three decades and enumeration units, Land, McCall, and Cohen (1990) found a consistent association in the expected direction at the state level, but not at lower levels of aggregation.

There is little empirical evidence of a relationship between age structure and police homicides. Five of the prior studies included an age structure variable and three found no evidence of a relationship with homicides (Fridell and Pate, 1995; Kaminski and Marvell, 2002;

Peterson and Bailey, 1994). Bailey and Peterson (1987) found a positive and statistically significant association in only one of twelve models estimated. Lott (2000) included an age variable, but estimates are not reported.

Police Educational Requirements

Educational level is commonly thought to be positively associated with police performance (Adler, Mueller, and Laufer, 1994:231; Armstrong and Polk, 1999). The belief that college-educated recruits make better officers probably began with August Vollmer in 1917, when he recruited university students to work part time for the Berkeley Police Department (Langworthy and Travis, 1997:86). Since then, administrators in favor of higher education have argued that college-educated officers write better reports, communicate better with the public, display more professionalism, use their discretion more wisely, make better decisions, are more sensitive to minority groups, and have fewer disciplinary problems (Adler, Mueller, and Laufer, 1994:231; Armstrong and Polk, 1999:67-71; Langworthy and Travis, 1997:87). However, it is not clear whether it is higher education itself or some other factor, such as motivation or intelligence, that accounts for both higher education and improved officer performance (Cascio, 1977:92).

Empirical Findings Regarding Police Educational Requirements

There is no empirical research on the relation of police education levels to officer homicide victimization, but education has been examined in studies of nonfatal assaults of police. Hale and Wilson (1974) found that officers with more education were more likely to be assaulted than officers with less education. However, a correlational study of 940 Dade County, Florida police officers found statistically significant inverse relationships between level of officer education and the number of: 1) assault-related injuries, 2) officer use-of-force reports, and 3) allegations of excessive use of force (Cascio, 1977: Table 1). Kaminski and Sorensen (1995:27) also found in a multivariate analysis of Baltimore County police that officers with four or more years of education were less likely to be injured when assaulted than officers with less than four years of education, and speculated that higher educational levels might be positively correlated with cautionary behaviors of officers.

Educational attainment may be associated with other behaviors that increase or decrease officer exposure to suspects and offenders. For instance, some research suggests that education is associated with police detection practices (e.g., vehicle stops) and arrest behavior (Riksheim and Chermak, 1993; Sherman, 1980a).

The likelihood of assault and injury may be related to education attainment, but the expected directions of the effects are unclear, particularly as it pertains to homicides of police. Thus, it seems reasonable to hypothesize that education may be related to victimization, though given the limited theoretical arguments and empirical evidence to date, it is best stated as nondirectional.

Police Agency Sex Stratification

The hiring of many more female police officers over the last couple of decades is described by Lott (2000:270) as a "massive experiment" in law enforcement, with two potential consequences. One is that increasing the number of females may have improved police effectiveness by drawing on "new untapped abilities;" the other is that effectiveness has declined because of the lowering of policing standards to allow the hiring of large numbers of women. Although there has been little empirical research on the increases in female police and risk of homicide victimization, historically there has been much debate over the safety of deploying women as patrol officers (Grennan, 1987:78; Hale and Wyland, 1993:1). According to Grennan (1987:78-79):

> The view of most police executives in the United States is that women, for the most part, do not belong on patrol because of their lack of physical strength and their inability to maintain an authoritarian presence in the face of challenges that the public can present to police officers. For the most part, the police managers' view is that female officers create a danger to other officers and to the public when they get involved in a violent situation.

Similarly, Hale and Wyland (1993:4) observe that male officers "still perceive police work as a man's domain where women will only get in the way, cannot be depended upon for backup, and may get hurt."

These perspectives suggest that increased hiring and deployment of woman as patrol officers not only increases the risk of victimization of female police, but that of male officers as well. If so, one would expect to observe a positive association between increases in the number of female officers employed and homicides of police.

An opposite perspective, however, is that female officers are just as competent as male officers in performing their duties, and that increased employment of female officers leads to reductions in police use of physical and deadly force (Hale and Wyland, 1993; Lonsway, 2001; *Police use of excessive force*, 1999; *Gender differences*, 2000; Peak, 1997:310). The National Center for Women in Policing (*Gender differences*, 2000:n.p.) summarizes this perspective well:

> More than 25 years of exhaustive research shows that women do the job of policing equally as well as men, responding to similar calls and encountering similar dangers. But more importantly, the research shows that women hold the key for substantially decreasing police violence and its cost. This new study confirms earlier research both in the United States and internationally that shows women police officers are less authoritarian, and rely less on physical force and more on verbal skills in handling altercations than their male counterparts. As a result, women police officers are better at defusing potentially violent confrontations with citizens and are less likely to become involved in problems with excessive force than male police officers.

Others reflect a similar position in stating that "the growing presence of women may help improve the tarnished image of policing, improve community relations, and foster a more flexible, less violent, approach to keeping the peace" (Peak, 1997:95). One Chief suggests that a "different touch, and possibly a softer image, will be given added weight in police departments" that hire more female officers, whereas another states "female officers have helped usher in a 'kindler, gentler organization'" (Ibid., 98).

This perspective suggests that increasing the number female officers may reduce the incidence of use of force, and by implication, violence against police. If so, one would expect to observe an inverse relationship between increases in the hiring of female officers and homicides of police.

The increased "feminization" of police forces may have a number of positive effects on police law enforcement agencies and the communities they serve, but some research provides indirect evidence that it may also produce some unintended consequences. Using a case-study approach, research on samples of law enforcement officers murdered or nearly murdered in the line of duty (N = 106) by the FBI ([Pinizzotto and Davis], 1992; Pinizzotto and Davis, 1997) found that most victim officers shared characteristics that seem similar to those attributed to female police by the National Center for Women in Policing (*Gender differences*, 2000). Most of the victim officers were described as friendly, well liked by the community, public relations and service-oriented, easy going, looked for good in others, used less force than other officers, and used force only as a last resort ([Pinizzotto and Davis], 1992:32; Pinizzotto and Davis, 1997:12). Although the FBI's sampling methodology has been criticized (King and Sanders, 1997), their results suggest that ushering in a "kindler, gentler organization" by recruiting greater numbers of female patrol officers could lead to increases in risk of officer victimization, and is worthy of exploration.

Empirical Findings Regarding Police Agency Sex Stratification

Regression-based studies have produced mixed results regarding the effects of police agency sex stratification. Depending on model specification, Lott found both negative and positive effects of the percentage of male officers on police homicides, but in neither regression were the effects statistically significant. Southwick (1998) found a positive and significant effect of increases over time in the percentage of male officers on the risk of police homicide, and offers several possible explanations. One is that males in the general population high in machismo self-select into police work and take greater risks on the job. Other explanations reflect notions of "chivalry", e.g., that criminals may be more reluctant to kill female officers, and that male officers partnered with female officers may be more cautious than those paired with male officers.

Lott (2000:241), however, suggests criminals may be *more* likely to attack female officers because females are physically weaker than males. Although he did not find a significant relationship with police homicides, Lott did find a positive and significant association between increases in the number of female officers employed in municipal police departments and nonfatal assaults on officers, suggesting that increasing women on patrol may increase the risk of attacks on police. Research on assault-related injuries, however, found no differences by officer sex (Grennan, 1987; Kaminski and Sorensen, 1995).

Given the conflicting perspectives and lack of consistent empirical findings regarding police sex stratification, a nondirectional hypothesis regarding the proportion of female police and risk of homicide victimization seems most appropriate.

ASSUMPTIONS

Before proceeding to the hypotheses, several assumptions regarding the opportunity model of police homicides need to be highlighted. First, it is assumed that the majority of police killers are at least minimally rational. The notion of rationality or bounded rationality on the part of motivated offenders is an important assumption of opportunity theory (Cornish and Clarke, 1986; Felson, 1998). Miethe, Stafford, and Long (1987:194), for example, indicate "criminal victimization occurs when motivated offenders in close proximity to potential victims make a rational selection of suitable targets who lack guardianship."

Although routine activities and lifestyle models have been used to explain both property and violent crime, Miethe, Stafford, and Long (1987:186) argue that because violent crimes are often expressive rather than instrumental acts, opportunity factors should exhibit a stronger relationship to property crime: "Hence, if motivated offenders engage in a conscious selection of suitable targets who lack guardianship, the spontaneous nature of most violent crimes is incongruent with the strictly rational characterization of human behavior underlying routine activity/lifestyle theories."

Cohen, Kluegel, and Land (1981:509) also argue that expressive rather than instrumental ends motivate assaults. This argument seems less relevant to murders of police, however, because most fatal assaults of police are committed by criminals perpetrating serious crimes who kill to avoid apprehension and punishment (Cardarelli, 1968; Creamer and Robin 1970 ; Margarita, 1980b), suggesting at least a minimal degree of rationality is involved in fatal attacks on police. This perspective is congruent with Cornish and Clarke's (1986:1) notion of bounded rationality, who argue "offenders seek to benefit themselves by their criminal behavior; that this involves the making of decisions and of choices, however rudimentary on occasion these processes might be; and that these processes exhibit a measure of rationality, albeit constrained by limits of time and ability and the availability of relevant information."

Rationality may often be present in offenses apparently pathologically motivated or carried out impulsively (Cornish and Clarke, 1986:2). Felson and Messner (1996:521), for example, state that although violent actions may appear to be impulsive and lacking of intent, they are instead "the result of quick and sometimes careless decision rather than involuntary behavior." More pointedly, harm is viewed "as a means to some end and all aggression as instrumental or goal-oriented action" (Ibid., 521).

Felson and Messner (1996:521) argue assailants are at least minimally aware of the "costs" imposed by potential targets and third parties. The perceived "net costs" are affected by the skills and resources of the protagonist(s) and antagonist(s) in an encounter, and such factors as "[r]elative physical size and strength, the possession of weapons, and the support of allies—all affect the power equation." The presence of third parties, in the case of police, might deter a potential assailant because of fear of identification, capture and punishment (Ibid., 522). Given these assumptions, Felson and Messner (1996:522-23) argue there are four motivating factors for homicides: 1) killing because of concerns for "justice and identity", e.g., when offenders have been humiliated by the victim; 2) killing for "practical reasons", e.g., such as when drug dealers kill other drug dealers to protect their business interests; 3) killing to avoid "target-imposed costs", e.g., to prevent the victim from retaliating or otherwise causing harm at a later time; and 4) killing to avoid costs imposed from third parties, e.g., killing potential witnesses who might otherwise identify the offender.

Most relevant to homicides of police are the avoidance of target-imposed costs (Cardarelli, 1968; Creamer and Robin, 1970; Margarita, 1980b). "The offender's goal is to avoid costs, a goal which may be well served by a lethal outcome. The lethal intent may be premeditated, or it may develop during the course of violent interaction" (Felson and Messner, 1996:523). Thus, the violence inflicted during murders of police is best conceived as instrumental aggression rather than angry aggression.

RATIONALITY AND TARGET SELECTION

There is an important difference between traditional criminal opportunity model target-selection processes and that assumed in the police homicide opportunity model proposed here. In the traditional model, at the level of the individual a rational offender may consider various factors, such as proximity to suitable targets, potential net yield or attractiveness, and degree of vulnerability or guardianship in choosing a suitable victim. Except in rare instances (psychopathic killers, politically motivated assassination), the officer-as-victim is unlikely to have been *chosen* per se, as most criminals would rather *avoid* detection by police. Rather than seeking out targets that are likely to provide monetary or other gain, it is assumed here that the decision-making process, however minimally rational, involves a determination by most criminals of various costs and benefits, including those associated with surrendering versus resisting if confronted by police. For example, prior to or upon detection, criminals may weigh the costs associated with giving up (e.g., personal safety, loss of freedom, reduced future income) against the costs (or benefits) associated with killing police (e.g., harsher sentence if caught and convicted, escape, reaping the rewards of the crime).

The opportunity model of police homicide victimization, then, assumes that the potential costs to the offender of being captured are in part determined by his or her prior criminal history, whether they are "wanted," and/or by the seriousness of the crime being committed when contact between the officer and offender occurs. The more serious the immediate crime and the more serious the offenders' criminal history, the greater will be the level of resistance by offenders, other factors being equal.

DETERMINANTS OF ORGANIZATIONAL DIFFERENCES IN WORKSTYLE

In the lifestyle-exposure model, individuals engage in leisure and work activities in an environment characterized by varying risks, i.e., there are "high-risk times, places and people" (Hindelang, Gottfredson, and Garofalo (1978:245), and differential exposure to these circumstances, situations, and persons influence patterns of victimization. Lifestyle differences among individuals and groups influence exposure to high-risk times, places and people, with lifestyle being the result of individual adaptations to role expectations and structural constraints (e.g., economic, familial, educational, legal). Similarly, in the opportunity model of police homicides, it is assumed that municipal government structure, local politics, unions, resource availability and allocation, and so on, influence police agency structure, policies, procedures, availability of equipment, and, to a degree, the way police perform their functions. As in the lifestyle-exposure model, however, these influences are unanalyzed.

SUMMARY

Miethe, Hughes, and McDowall (1991:166) state "changes in conventional activities increase crime rates because they increase exposure to motivated offenders, enhance target attractiveness, or decrease the level of guardianship." Similarly, the opportunity model of police homicide victimization predicts that changes or variation in police activities and crime levels impact risk of officer victimization. Specifically, it is expected that differences across agencies in deployment patterns, departmental policies and police practices, and variation in the pool of motivated offenders across jurisdictions influence opportunities for homicides of police.

Hypotheses are provided in the next section, and the operationalization of variables appears in Chapter 4. Note, however, that operationalizing opportunity model concepts such exposure, attractiveness and exposure traditionally has been difficult (Hough, 1987). Frequently, empirical measures used represent multiple concepts, and thus have ambiguous meanings (Miethe, Hughes, and McDowall, 1991:168). For example, although "criminal opportunity and social disorganization theories are substantively distinct, it is impossible in many cases to distinguish empirical tests of them because of the way major concepts have been measured" (Ibid., 167). Income may indicate attractiveness or reduced criminal motivations, while unemployment may indicate criminogenic conditions that increase criminal motivations or reduced levels of nonhousehold leisure activities that reduce criminal opportunities; "proper examination of how each theoretical component influences crime rates requires adequate controls for other relevant variables and the various dimensions of each concept" (Ibid., 168). But whether, say, income and unemployment increase/decrease crime through their impact on opportunities or criminal motivations is not critical for the present analysis, as the interest in this study is in the net effect of such factors on the size of the pool of motivated offenders, and in turn, how the size of this pool affects opportunities for contact between offenders and police.

An additional limitation of the study is that the major concepts of opportunity theory themselves are not measured uniquely (proximity, exposure, attractiveness and guardianship). This also has been a limitation of many tests of opportunity theory. Miethe, Hughes, and McDowall (1991:168) for instance, note that some studies have used the household-activity ratio, which represents the concepts of exposure, attractiveness and guardianship. In most cases, unique measures of the various theoretical concepts are not available, nor are various dimensions of certain concepts measured (e.g., the economic and symbolic dimensions of attractiveness). Despite these limitations, available data do allow the testing of many variables and hypothesized relationships that are consistent with opportunity theory.

HYPOTHESES

Based on the above discussion, 14 hypotheses are generated. The first four pertain to indicators of proximity to motivated offenders, three of which are factor scores derived from a principal components analysis (discussed in Chapter 5). Hypotheses 5 and 6 pertain to exposure to motivated offenders, and hypotheses 7 through 11 pertain to guardianship. The final three hypotheses (12-14) pertain to the control variables, two of which are nondirectional.

1) Proximity

$H_{\circledR 1}$ Resource deprivation will be positively related to homicides of police.

$H_{\circledR 2}$ Population density will be positively related to homicides of police.

$H_{\circledR 3}$ Residential stability will be inversely related to homicides of police.

$H_{\circledR 4}$ Field officer density will be positively related to homicides of police.

2) Exposure

$H_{\circledR 5}$ The number of arrests for Part I crimes will be positively related to homicides of police.

$H_{\circledR 6}$ The percentage of sworn officers assigned to foot patrol will be positively related to homicides of police.

3) Guardianship

$H_{\circledR 7}$ The percentage of sworn officers assigned to one-officer patrol units will be positively related to homicides of police.

$H_{\circledR 8}$ Mandatory bulletproof vest-wear policies will be inversely related to homicides of police.

$H_{\circledR 9}$ Agency authorization of personal-issue chemical agents for field officers will be inversely related to homicides of police.

$H_{\circledR 10}$ Agency authorization or issuance of semiautomatic sidearms to field officers will be inversely related to homicides of police.

$H_{\circledR 11}$ The number of hours of academy training required for new recruits will be inversely related to homicides of police.

4) Controls

$H_{\circledR 12}$ The percentage of sworn female officers will be related to homicides of police.

$H_{\circledR 13}$ Agency location in the South will be positively related to homicides of police.

$H_{\circledR 14}$ Agency educational requirements will be related to homicides of police.

CHAPTER 2

Literature Review

HISTORICAL OVERVIEW

Police homicides have been the subject of academic study since at least the 1930s, when Brearley (1934) compared the numbers of police murdered during the 1920s across several cities. Most of the early research on homicides of police, though, was conducted in the 1960s following the publication by the FBI of national statistics on law enforcement officers killed in the line of duty. These studies, however, were exclusively descriptive in nature, examining locations, weapons used, type of assignment, and the circumstances surrounding murders of police (Bristow, 1970; Cardarelli, 1968; Chapman, 1972, Creamer and Robin, 1970). Although informative at the time, researchers were unable to collect base-rate information, that is, an appropriate denominator, and therefore were limited in their ability to accurately attribute risk of victimization to particular calls for service, types of assignment, locations, and so on (Garner and Clemmer, 1986; Sherman, 1980b:8).

The 1970s witnessed an incremental increase in the methodological sophistication of research on homicides of police, when the first correlational studies were conducted using states and cities as the units of analysis. Much of the research during this decade and in the early 1980s was not guided by theory, however, and along with large numbers of other correlates several highly questionable variables were included with little or no explication (Lester, 1978a, 1978b, 1980, 1982). Examples include latitude/longitude, percent voting for Nixon, elevation above sea level, and mean annual temperature (Lester, 1978a; 1978b).

Studies on police killings in the early 1980s still lacked base-rate information, and continued to be descriptive or correlational (Geller and Karales 1982; Konstantin 1984; Little 1984; Margarita 1980a, 1980b, 1980c). An exception was William Bailey (1982), who advanced research on police homicides by estimating the first cross-sectional multiple linear regression model using states as the unit of analysis. Using similar methods, data, and models, William Bailey and Ruth Peterson dominated the study of macro-level influences on police homicides throughout the 1980s (Bailey and Peterson, 1987; Peterson and Bailey, 1988). In the early 1990s they conducted the first (monthly) time series analysis of homicides of police (Peterson and Bailey, 1994). With the exception of their study that sought to determine whether various structural characteristics of states influenced homicide rates of police and civilians similarly (Peterson and Bailey, 1988), the focus of their research was to assess the deterrent effects of the death penalty on police homicides while controlling for social, demographic, and economic influences (Bailey, 1982; Bailey and Peterson, 1997; Peterson and Bailey, 1994).

Around the same time Chamlin (1989) and Fridell and Pate (1995) also studied the influence of structural conditions on police homicides, with the latter being the first study to use cities as the unit of analysis in a multiple regression model. Chamlin (1989) conceptualized his analysis from a conflict perspective, though the regressors used in his models are also those commonly used in social disorganization and strain theoretic approaches.

Recently, Jacobs and Carmichael (2002), Kaminski and Marvell (2002), Lott (2000), and Southwick (1998), employed more sophisticated analytical techniques to model police killings. Jacobs and Carmichael (2002) estimated a series of Poisson and negative binomial cross-section regression models using 165 cities as the unit of analysis. The primary interest was to determine whether the presence of a black mayor was associated with a reduced risk of police homicide while controlling for a variety of other social, demographic and economic conditions.

Kaminski and Marvell (2002) conducted annual time series analyses to determine whether structural conditions and other factors influenced police and general homicides similarly. Unlike Peterson and Bailey (1988), however, who used a series of cross-sectional models and "eyeballed" regression estimates across models to determine whether structural characteristics of states produced similar effects, Kaminski and Marvell used Chow tests to test the significance of coefficients across separate time-series regressions.

Lott (2000), interested in whether increased hiring of female and black police officers decreased police performance (crime rates), also examined their impacts on police homicides and assaults on police across 174 cities and three time periods using two-stage least squares and fixed-effects linear panel regression models.

Finally, Southwick (1998) tested the effects of percentage male police, police wages, and number of guns per capita on the risk of police homicide using regression time series analyses and two-stage least squares.

As this brief historical overview indicates, the statistical methodologies employed in macro-level research on police homicides have continually advanced over the last several decades. As is evident in the detailed review of studies to follow, however, most of the research has concentrated on the adverse effects of economic strains (e.g., poverty, income inequality, unemployment), weak social controls (e.g., population size and density, racial and ethnic heterogeneity, family disruption), and crime or on the effects of capital punishment while controlling for economic strains and weak social controls.

The implicit assumption often has been that higher aggregate levels of economic distress and community disorganization increase levels of crime and violence that in turn increase levels of violence against police. In other words, the focus of the extant macro-level research has been on the factors that free persons to engage in crime or that generate criminal motivations, with little consideration given to other factors that influence opportunities for the victimization of police officers.

REVIEW OF SPECIFIC STUDIES

This section provides a detailed review of the 10 previous studies of police homicides employing multiple regression. Table 2.1 provides a summary of the findings. Included in the table are the names of the researchers, the time periods examined, publication dates, the regressors examined, whether regressors were statistically significant, and the direction of effects.

Bailey (1982) and Bailey and Peterson (1987; 1994) conducted research to assess the deterrent effects of statutory provisions for the death penalty and executions on homicides of police controlling for a variety of structural conditions. The first two studies used states as the unit of analysis, while the third was a national time series. In the first of these studies, Bailey (1982) applied OLS regression in annual cross-sections for the years 1961-1971. Bailey and Peterson (1987) employed the same methods to study homicides of police during 1973-1984. Both studies controlled for a number of structural and crime variables, and included lagged effects in the models. Neither study found support for a deterrent effect of capital punishment on killings of police, nor were consistent effects observed for any of the structural and crime regressors examined (racial composition, poverty level, unemployment rate, urbanicity, sex ratio, region, percent aged 15-34, violent crime, property crime, and total index crime).[7]

To test whether executions and media coverage of executions deter police killers, Bailey and Peterson (1994) estimated a monthly time series regression for the years 1976-1989. Controlling for percent metropolitan population, percent African-American population, percent aged 16-34, divorce rate, unemployment rate and percent recipients of aid for families with dependent children, the authors found no evidence that executions or associated media coverage deter murders of police. Among the structural regressors, only percent African-American (inversely associated) and divorce rate (positively associated) were significantly related to police homicides (rate per 100,000 law enforcement employees). These effects were statistically insignificant, however, when the authors reestimated their model with all variables differenced, i.e., when month-to-month *changes* in the independent variables were examined.[8]

Interested in whether homicides of police are influenced by the same structural factors that explain civilian homicides, Peterson and Bailey (1988) examined murders of law enforcement officers for the years 1977-1984, employing the same methods used in their previous two cross-sectional studies. Like their earlier findings, no consistent predictors of police homicides were identified (regressors were the divorce rate, percent below poverty, percent black, racial income inequality, income inequality residual, percent metropolitan population, location in the South, and residuals of the total, violent, and property crime rates).[9] Most variables, however, were associated with general homicide rates in each year, the exceptions being racial income inequality and region. Their results suggest police murderers and murderers in general do not respond similarly to the same structural conditions.

In their reexamination of this research question, Kaminski and Marvell (2002:703) comment on Peterson and Bailey's (1988) study, arguing that "one cannot conclude that the impacts are different just because a coefficient is significant in one regression but not in another, especially with a small sample of 50 observations, because the difference between coefficients might not be significant." Using an alternative source of data on police killings from the National Law Enforcement Officers Memorial Fund, Kaminski and Marvell (2002) estimate annual time series models to test whether the same structural factors affect police and total homicides similarly for the years 1930 – 1998.

For police homicides, the authors found that prison populations and involvement in WWII for the years 1943-1944 were inversely related to murders of police, while the divorce rate was positively related. Certain economic factors (income and inflation, but not unemployment or consumer prices) were significantly associated in the expected direction. Age structure (percent 15-17, 18-24, 25-34, and 35-44), executions, a "crack years" variable,[10] firearm use (percent total homicides by firearm), trauma systems[11] and measures of police body armor usage[12] were unrelated to police killings.

Comparing these results to a model for total homicides using the same regressors, the authors conclude (with the exceptions of crack cocaine, age structure and divorce) the factors that explain trends in homicide generally also explain trends in police killings, though their impacts on police homicides usually were larger. They suggest that economic growth, inflation decline, prison population growth, and World War II affect criminals' motivation and availability to commit crime, but speculate that because police come into contact with criminals more often than most citizens, criminals have more opportunities to assault police. Therefore, the effects of the regressors on homicides of police are magnified.

Espousing a conflict perspective of crime control to explain violence against police, Chamlin (1989) tested whether, independent of structural covariates, the presence of "threatening populations" (the poor and minorities) was positively associated with slayings of law enforcement officers. Estimating six models using OLS and ridge regression to analyze the rate of police homicides at the state level aggregated over three years (1980-1982), this study failed to identify consistent predictors of homicides of police (regressors examined were arrest rate, Index crime rate, rate of FTE sworn officers, the divorce rate, percent Black, percent with Spanish surnames, poverty, and income inequality).[13]

In one of only three studies using cities as the unit of analysis (N = 56), Fridell and Pate (1995) employed OLS regression to analyze the impacts of structural and crime-related variables on homicides of police for the years 1977-1992. Because they observed a decline in the rate of police homicides after 1984, Fridell and Pate estimated separate regression models for the years 1977-1984 and 1985-1992. The only statistically significant regressor across both models was the violent crime rate (other variables examined were region, poverty, racial composition, population density, population aged 15-34, property crime rate, a gun crime index, property and violent crime arrest rates, and the percent of police assault-related injuries).[14]

Estimating a time-series model and a system of four equations using two-stage least squares, Southwick (1998) examined three factors thought to be associated with the risk of being killed feloniously in the line of duty nationally for the years 1961 – 1993.[15] Regressors were police real wages,[16] the percentage of sworn male officers, and total guns per capita. The author found that the risk of being murdered was positively associated with the percentage of male police officers and inversely associated with real wages, whereas total guns per capita was unrelated to the risk of being killed. Southwick (1998:604) concludes that reducing the proportion of male officers will reduce police homicide risk and that "police who are paid more will have an incentive to work more safely and, in fact, will act so as to reduce their actual risk as a result of their increased demand for life."

Interested primarily in the effects of increases in the numbers of female and minority police officers hired on police performance (Index crime rates), Lott (2000) examined as well their influence on homicides of police in 174 cities for the years 1987, 1990, and 1993 using two-stage weighted least squares to first estimate the impact of consent decrees on the hiring of females and minorities (including a number of controls). In the second stage he estimated the effects of the percentage male, black, and minority officers on the rate of police assaulted and murdered. In these regressions he controlled for city demographic characteristics (age structure, race, sex),[17] the average weekly wage, the unemployment rate, population size, and the per capita number of sworn officers, but does not report coefficients for these regressors. Lott estimates each model twice; once with city and year fixed effects, and a second time with county fixed effects and separate year fixed effects for each state. When using city and year fixed effects, the percentage of the force that is black is inversely related to murders of police, but is statistically insignificant. When using county fixed effects and separate year fixed effects for each state, percent black is significant and positive. Similar results are obtained when the percent minority is used in place of percent black. The percentage male is not statistically significant in either model. He subsequently adds an indicator of the presence of a mandatory vest-wear policy, but it was insignificant in all models. Lott (2000:258) concludes, "it is difficult to see any consistent pattern for the killing of police officers . . . though this might arise because these deaths are so infrequent."

Finally, Jacobs and Carmichael (2002) use Poisson and negative binomial cross-section regression models to test political influences on murders of police across 165 cities with 1980 populations greater than 100,000. Adopting a conflict perspective, the primary interest in this study is whether the presence of a black mayor reduces blacks' inclinations to murder police when controlling for levels of violent crime and a variety of other social, economic, and demographic factors.

To construct their dependent variables, the authors aggregated FBI police homicide data for the years 1981 – 1990. The number of sworn officers per police department is used to adjustment for unequal exposure in their regression models.[18] A series of regression models are estimated controlling for population size, the ratio of black to white median household income, percent black population, growth in percent black population 1970 to 1980, economic inequality, residential segregation, percent below poverty, percent unemployed, percent divorced, percent female-headed black households, percent female-headed white households, percent of dwellings with more than 1.01 person per room (crowding), region, violent crime rate, civilian murder rate, robbery rate, and the rate of police killings of blacks 1980 – 1986.[19]

The results show consistent support for the authors' main hypothesis, i.e., that police officers are significantly less likely to be fatally assaulted in cities with a black mayor (only 11 cities had a black mayor in 1980). The authors interpret this finding as evidence that murders of police reflect partially a form of primitive political rebellion, even if the killers are unable to "justify their acts with political concepts" (Jacobs and Carmichael, 1229: 2002). But as Jacobs and Carmichael point out, they are unable to ascertain the motives of the murderers due to the aggregate nature of their study. Other evidence, however, suggests that rather than being politically or racially motivated to kill police, most offenders murder police because they wish to avoid apprehension and punishment (Cardarelli, 1968; Creamer and Robin, 1970 ; Margarita, 1980b; [Pinizzotto and Davis, 1992]).

Based on this review it is clear that the extant research on police homicides has produced mixed findings. None of the predictors examined consistently exhibit a significant association with killings of police across studies, and the directions of some effects are opposite that expected (e.g., violent crime, population density, income inequality). Among the majority of covariates examined, null findings are the rule rather than the exception, casting substantial doubt on whether such factors are capable of explaining cross-unit variation in police killings. In summary, the ability of prior research to explain cross-unit or temporal variation in felonious killings of law enforcement officers has been disappointing.

LIMITATIONS OF THE PREVIOUS RESEARCH

The prior research can be criticized primarily on two grounds. These are the narrowness or lack of theory (but see Jacobs and Carmichael, 2002) and model specification issues. Most studies lacked theory to guide analysis or theory was only marginally explicated. Further, many potentially important opportunity factors were not included. If opportunity factors are important for explaining homicides of police but are excluded, extant models are misspecified.

Regarding other specification issues, Land, McCall, and Cohen (1990:934) argue that among the methodological hazards of area-based analyses, the "most insidious of these pertain to the influence of multicollinearity on the substantive inference that can be drawn from partialling in regression analysis." In their review of methodological issues in ecological research on civilian homicides, they summarize the potential adverse effects of collinearity among regressors. These are instability of regression estimates (large changes in estimates when a variable or observation is added or deleted), wide confidence intervals, nonsignificant test statistics, and algebraic signs opposite of theoretical expectations.

Like much of the research on homicide generally, multicollinearity is an issue for many of the studies on police homicides. Bailey (1982), Kaminski and Marvell (2002), Lott (2000), and Southwick (1998), for example, do not mention conducting tests for multicollinearity among regressors (though the time series studies do address the issue of autocorrelation). Fridell and Pate (1995) combined certain variables that were likely highly collinear (poverty, percent black, Gini Index), but apparently conducted no tests for collinearity among the remaining regressors in their models. Similarly, Bailey and Peterson (1987:15, note 11) and Bailey and Peterson (1994:64) test for collinearity among *death penalty* regressors, but not among other covariates. In their 1988 study, Peterson and Bailey (1988:229) indicate in a footnote that they found no evidence of collinearity problems, but they provide no details on how they tested for multicollinearity. Chamlin (1989) used ridge regression to address the problem of multicollinearity, but ridge regression is not necessarily an improvement over OLS in the presence of multicollinearity (Kennedy, 1992:185-186; Pedhauzer, 1982:247). Based on reported variance inflation factors only, Jacobs and Carmichael (2002) found no strong evidence of multicollinearity, though even in this study the tests for collinearity were limited.[20]

Thus, many of the substantive inferences regarding the independent effects of regressors drawn from the previous research on police homicides may suffer due to multicollinearity. In addition, it appears that only Chamlin (1989) conducted additional regression diagnostics, such as analysis of residuals and influential cases (though Kaminski and Marvell (2002) and Lott (2000) do report conducting many alternative regressions using different model specifications).

Another potentially serious specification issue in most studies relates to the nature of the dependent variable. Felonious killings of law enforcement officers are exceptionally rare events. The FBI reports, for instance, that 42 officers were murdered in the Nation during 1999 (*Law enforcement officers killed and assaulted*, 2000). This is an average of fewer than two officers murdered per state, and many states have zero police homicides in any given year. Thus the distribution of these events at the state or lower level of aggregation cannot be considered normal or continuous, an important assumption of the linear model. Although use of the linear model to analyze event counts may be reasonable when the mean of the counts is large (Cameron and Trivedi 1998:2), this is unlikely to be the case regarding police homicides. Under these conditions, use of the linear model can result in biased, inefficient, and inconsistent estimates (Long 1997:217). With the exception of Jacobs and Carmichael (2002), the studies listed in Table 2.1 used linear methods to analyze homicides of police. Thus, inferences regarding the effects of the independent variables in many of the studies may be erroneous.

An additional limitation of the prior research is that all but one study calculated police homicide rates using the number of sworn police, but not all sworn police are deployed in the field and thus "at risk" or the risk is nearly nonexistent for those not deployed in the field.[21] Although one might expect the total number sworn and the number of field officers to correlate highly, the proportion of sworn officers assigned to field duties varies substantially across police departments.[22] Using the number of sworn officers in calculating estimates of risk, therefore, may be problematic for cross-agency or cross-jurisdictional analyses.

Lastly, though perhaps not a major criticism, several cross-sectional studies of homicides of police used states as the unit of analysis (Bailey, 1982; Bailey and Peterson, 1987; Chamlin, 1989; Peterson and Bailey, 1988). Because states combine vastly different ecological units (e.g., rural areas and large cities) and substantial intra-unit variability in homicide rates and structural conditions are ignored, it is arguable that cities constitute a more appropriate unit of analysis (Bailey, 1984; Chamlin, 1989; Kovandzic, Vieraitis and Yeisley, 1998). In any case, since only three studies have used cities when analyzing police homicides (Fridell and Pate, 1995; Jacobs and Carmichael, 2002; Lott, 2000), the present study adds to the research conducted at this level of analysis by including many city-level structural regressors (some previously unexamined).

Table 2.1: Variables used in prior multiple regression analyses of homicides of police

Source	Unit/Period	Method	Social Control/Disorganization		Strain/Deprivation		Other	
Bailey (1982)	States 1961-1971	OLS; 11 annual cross sections	Urban Executions	ns ns	Poverty (2 / 11) Unemploy. (3 / 11) Nonwhite (2 / 11)	+ + +		
Bailey & Peterson (1987)	States 1973-1984	OLS; 12 annual cross sections	Age (1/12) Executions	+ ns	Poverty(6/ 12) Black (2/12) Sex Ratio (5/12)	+ –/+ –/+	South(2/12) Violent crime Property crime Index crime	+ ns ns ns
Peterson & Bailey (1988)	States 1977-1984	OLS; 8 annual cross sections	Divorce (2/8) Urban	+ ns	Poverty (2/8) Gini Racial Gini Black	+ ns	South Homicide crime Violent crime Property crime Index crime	+ ns ns ns ns
Chamlin (1989)	States 1980-1982	OLS & ridge; 6 cross section models	Divorce (3/6)	+	Poverty (2/3) Gini (1/3) Black (1/3) Hispanic (3/6)	+ – + +	Index crimes (3/6) Index arrests Sworn cops (2/6)	– ns –

59

continued

Table 2.1, continued

Source	Unit/Period	Method	Social Control/ Disorganization	Strain/ Deprivation	Other
Peterson & Bailey (1994)	National 1976-1989	OLS; monthly time series	Divorced + Urban ns Age ns Executions ns Executions in Media ns	Unemployment ns Black – Welfare ns	
Fridell & Pate (1995)	56 Cities 1977-1984 & 1985-1992	OLS; 2 cross section models	Density ns Age ns	Poverty index ns/– Hispanic ns Income ns	South ns Violent crime +/+ Property crime +/ns Gun crime +/ns Violent arrests –/ns Property arrests +/ns Assaults of cops ns
Southwick (1998)	National 1961-1993	Time series			# Guns ns Male cops + Police wages –
Lott (2000)	174 Cities 1987, 1990, 1993	2SLS weighted OLS; city, county & year fixed effects panel	Age nr Population nr	Black nr Hispanic nr Other race nr Male nr Unemployment nr Income nr	Black cops ns/+ Minority cops –/+ Male cops ns Mandatory vest policy ns

60

Source	Unit/Period	Method	Social Control/ Disorganization	Strain/ Deprivation	Other
Kaminski & Marvell (2002)	National 1930-1998	Time series, SUR; 2 models	Age — ns Divorce — ns/+ Prison pop — -/- WWII 42-45 — ns WWII 43-44 — -/- Executions — ns	Unemployment — ns Income — -/+ Consumer prices — +/ns CPI levels — ns/+ Inflation — ns/+	Trauma systems — ns Firearms use — ns Body armor use — ns Crack years — ns
Jacobs & Carmichael (2002)	165 Cities 1980	Poisson &negative binomial; 10 cross section models	Population (10/10) — + Population density (10/10) — ns Divorce (10/10) — + Female-headed black family (0/1) Female-headed white family (0/1)	Black (2/10) — + Blk growth (8/8) — + Blk-white median income (10/10) — - Gini (0/1) — ns Poverty (0/1) — ns Segregation (9/10) — - Unemployment (0/1) Crowding (0/1)	South — ns Midwest — ns Northeast — ns Black mayor (9/9) — - Violent Crime (9/9) — + Robbery (1/1) — ns Murder (1/1) — + Police killings of blks — ns Blk x pop (8/8) — +

Note: Numbers in parentheses indicate the number of models in which regressors were found significant when there were more than two models; nr = nor reported; ns = not significant; + = positive association; – =negative association; - = positive association; OLS = ordinary least squares; 2SLS = two-stage least squares; SUR = seemingly unrelated regression.

CHAPTER 3

Data and Operationalization of Variables

This chapter discusses the sources of data used in the analysis and several issues pertaining to the dependent and independent variables. The operationalization of variables appears at the end of the chapter. Data for the analysis come from four sources. Agency-level data on arrests and offenses known to the police are from the Federal Bureau of Investigation's (FBI) *Uniform Crime Reporting* (UCR) program. These data are monthly counts of the number of Index offenses known and arrests recorded and reported by police agencies to the FBI's UCR program each year. Offenses known to police include reports of Index crimes (excluding arson) received from victims, officers who discovered infractions, or other sources (U.S. Department of Justice, 2000). Non-Index arrest data include counts for 43 offenses, disaggregated by arrestee age, sex, and race (Chilton and Weber, 2000), but for reasons explained earlier only arrests for crime Index offenses are used in the analysis. Electronic data for arrests and offenses known were obtained from the National Archive of Criminal Justice Data (NACJD) maintained by the Inter-university Consortium for Political and Social Research (ICPSR) (www.icpsr.umich.edu/NACJD).

Electronic data on the organization of municipal police departments are from the Law Enforcement Management and Administrative Statistics (LEMAS) (U.S. Department of Justice, 1996a, 1996b, 1997, 1999), and also were obtained from the NACJD data archive. The LEMAS survey, administered by the Bureau of the Census for the Bureau of Justice Statistics (BJS), collects limited information from nationally representative samples of publicly funded State and local law enforcement agencies with fewer than 100 sworn officers, and more complete information on all State and local law enforcement agencies employing 100 or more sworn officers (135 in 1987). Data collection began in 1987, with additional administrations of the questionnaire occurring approximately every three years thereafter. For each survey, the pay period containing June 15 is used as the reference date for personnel-related questions, and June 30 for other questions (Reaves and Smith, 1995).

The LEMAS data used in the analysis are from the 1987, 1990, 1993, and 1997 administrations of the survey. The departments included for study are those classified by BJS as municipal departments employing 100 or more sworn officers in 1990 serving populations of 100,000 or larger (N = 190). A listing of agency jurisdictions (cities) is provided in Table A1 in the Appendix. Data from the other waves were matched to the 1990 data using Originating Agency Identifier (ORI) codes, which are unique agency identifiers assigned to individual law enforcement agencies by the FBI for data reporting purposes.

Bureau of the Census data for 1990 were obtained from two sources: the Missouri State Census Data Center archive at http://mcdc.missouri.edu/applications/uexplore.html and the National Consortium on Violence Research site at http://www.ncovr.heinz. cmu.edu. Census data from 1990 are used because they are most proximate in time to the LEMAS data (Census 2000 data were not available at the time of data processing).

The various datasets were merged using the *Law Enforcement Agency Identifiers Crosswalk* data file developed by BJS and the NACJD (U.S. Department of Justice, Bureau of Justice Statistics, 2000). This file contains ORI codes, Federal Information Processing Standards (FIPS) codes, and Government Identification (GOVID) codes that allow for easy matching of UCR crime data for police agencies to Census data for their respective government entities (Lindgren and Zawitz, 2001). The electronic crosswalk file was obtained from the NACJD archive at www.icpsr.umich.edu/NACJD/.

Data on police homicides were obtained directly from hard-copy narratives of incidents as reported in the FBI's *Law Enforcement Officers Killed and Assaulted* (1998 and earlier years) *Summaries of Incidents*. These narratives identify the departments that employed the victim officers, the date and time of the assault, the date of death, whether more than one officer was slain, and other details surrounding the incidents.[23]

DATA ISSUES: THE DEPENDENT VARIABLE

Because homicides of police are extremely rare and fluctuate widely over time, three-year counts (sums) are taken around the years 1987, 1990, 1993, and 1996 (see, e.g., Morenoff, Sampson, and Raudenbush, 2001). For example, the data for 1990 is the sum of the number of homicide incidents that occurred in 1989, 1990 and 1991. For the period 1985–1997, 239 officers were murdered in 233 incidents. Although the dependent variable is the number of *incidents*, 98.7 percent of the incidents involved a single victim. Thus, for practical purposes, the outcome may be thought of as the *number* of sworn officers murdered, and for ease of explication it is frequently referred to as such.

The police homicide data compiled by the FBI are considered to be highly reliable and valid (Chapman, 1998:8; Margarita 1980a:16). Homicides of police are the most widely publicized events in law enforcement, and when assailants remain at large all law enforcement agencies are notified, including the FBI, with the hope that the perpetrator will be apprehended. When local police apprehend a suspect, at a minimum the FBI is notified to access the suspect's criminal history file prior to trial (Chapman, 1998:8; Konstantin 1984:34).

In addition to receiving notification of duty-related deaths directly from state and local law enforcement agencies, the FBI receives notification from its field divisions and legal attaché officers, and from the Public Safety Officers' Benefits Program (administered by the Bureau of Justice Assistance). Once notification has been made, the FBI obtains additional details concerning the circumstances surrounding the death from the victim officer's employing agency. The primary source of error is the rare incident where the cause of death is not clearly identified (Konstantin 1984:34).

Although police homicide data suffer from very little measurement error, it may nevertheless be beneficial to construct a dependent variable that incorporates serious but nonfatal assaults. A reasonable argument can be made that there exists substantial overlap between the "structure, intention and motivational background of most serious but nonfatal attacks and most homicides," and that in many instances chance alone plays a significant role as to whether an assault becomes a homicide (Zimring 1972:110). Including both homicides and serious but nonfatal attacks, therefore, may more closely represent the "true" level of serious violence directed against police.

It may be especially appropriate to count the number of incidents in which police are shot at, as it seems reasonably clear that the assailant's intent is to kill or cause an officer grave harm. Cardarelli (1968:447) argues, for instance, that having information on the number of times police were shot at provides a more meaningful measure of the potential danger police encounter on the job.

Furthermore, because murders of police are rare events, an added benefit of including serious but nonfatal assaults in the dependent variable would be to increase substantially the number of incidents for analysis. Research by Geller and Karales (1982:343) in Chicago found that of 105 police officers intentionally shot at during 1974 – 1978, only 15 (14%) were struck (six fatally). From 1971 – 1975, Fyfe (1979:320) found that of 844 officers New York City sustaining line-of-duty injuries in firearms discharge/assault incidents, only 30 (3.6%) were killed. Margarita (1980a:158) found that 75 percent of the shots fired at police missed, and that a hit was fatal less than 1 out of 12 times. These findings suggest that reliance on only fatalities substantially underestimates the degree of serious violence directed at police.

Unfortunately, incorporating the number of serious assaults or even the number of officers wounded by firearms into the dependent variable would introduce substantial measurement error. The 1997 national nonfatal police assault data reported by the FBI are based on 8,692 participating law enforcement agencies supplying figures for all 12 months of that year (Law enforcement officers killed and assaulted, 1997:1). Since there were approximately 19,000 state and local law enforcement agencies in the United States in 1997 (Reaves and Goldberg, 2000:28), the agencies that volunteer to report these data represent fewer than 50 percent of the population of agencies. In addition, among those serving populations of 100,000 or more, the FBI reports 204 participating municipal, county and state agencies in 1997 (Law enforcement officers killed and assaulted, 1997:2), while the Bureau of Justice Statistics reports over 242 local agencies serving populations of 100,000 or more (Reaves and Goldberg, 2000:3,Table 3).[24] Therefore, nonfatal assault data for some number of large municipal agencies are likely unavailable.

Furthermore, of the agencies that report nonfatal assaults to the FBI, some fail to report all attacks, and the assault data that are provided from different jurisdictions suffer from definitional inconsistencies (Margarita, 1980c:225). However, it may be assumed that as the level of the seriousness of assaults on police increase, the reliability and validity of the data improve (Margarita, 1980a:53). Because almost all police are killed by firearms (Law enforcement officers killed and assaulted, 1998), one reasonably might use *injurious assaults by firearm* as a component of a measure of violence against police.

To investigate this possibility, the number of officers injured by firearm in 1997 for municipal agencies serving cities with populations of 100,000 or greater was examined using Law Enforcement Officers Killed and Assaulted (LEOKA) data obtained from the NACJD archive at www.icpsr.umich.edu/NACJD/ (U.S. Department of Justice, 1999). These data, however, show substantial nonreporting and underreporting of incidents, and therefore are of questionable utility, particularly for cross-agency analyses. One is left with the choice of using conceptually more appealing but less reliable and valid data to construct the dependent variable, or using the highly reliable and valid fatality data. The choice here is to follow prior practice by using homicides.

DATA ISSUES: INDEPENDENT VARIABLES

As noted earlier, LEMAS data used in the analysis are from the 1987, 1990, 1993 and 1997 surveys. The referent period for some questions (e.g., calls for service), however, is from July 1 of the previous year through June 30 of the current year. Thus, "1993" data are comprised of information referring to the last six months of 1992 (July 1 – December 31) plus the first six months of 1993 (January 1 – June 30). For certain survey items the referent date is June 30. As an example, respondents are asked to indicate the number of full-time employees assigned to field operations during the pay period that included June 30. Many questions, though, do not have a specific referent date. For instance, the 1993 survey asks simply "How many hours of training does your agency require for new officers recruits?" Information regarding patrol types is sought for the "most recent week available" (see Reaves and Smith, 1995:289-296). Thus, for these questions it is assumed the data reflect operations sometime during 1993.

Because some new survey questions were added with each administration of the LEMAS survey, not all variables used in the analysis are available in all waves of data. For example, the percentage of officers in one-unit patrols and the percentage of officers on foot patrol are available for 1993 and 1997 but not for 1987 and 1990;

information on agency authorization of chemical agents and mandatory vest-wear policies is available in all waves but 1987. In addition, the wording of certain questions changed with subsequent versions of the survey. In 1990, agencies were asked whether they authorized chemical agents, but pepper spray was not specified until 1993. Thus, not all variables are directly comparable across waves. Specific referent periods and differences in wording of items across administrations of the survey are made explicit in the variable operationalization section at the end of this chapter.

A further concern regarding the LEMAS data is that not all agencies responded to each question in every wave. Where possible, one of two procedures was used to fill in missing data, depending on whether data were continuous (e.g., number of field officers) or dichotomous (e.g., presence/absence of a mandatory vest-wear policy). If the value for a continuous variable was missing for an agency in a particular wave, a value from an adjacent wave was substituted (a *subsequent* year was used first if available, or a *prior* year if not available). If data from an immediately adjacent year was not available, a value from the next adjacent wave was used.[25]

Decisions regarding missing data for dichotomous variables were more complicated, and Table 3.1 shows an example of the decision rules used for handling missing data for dichotomous variables available across three waves (e.g., mandatory vest-wear policy).[26] The same logic, however, applies to dichotomous variables available in all four waves that have missing data (e.g., authorization/issuance of semi-automatic sidearms).

Two kinds of crime data from the UCR are used for the analysis. These are the total number of Part I offenses known to the police and the total number of persons arrested for Part I offenses, excluding arson (murder and nonnegligent manslaughter, forcible rape, robbery, aggravated assault, burglary, larceny-theft, and motor vehicle theft).

Although complete data were available for most agencies in most years, not all agencies in the sample reported 12 months of data. For these cases, data were imputed for a full year using the formula

$$C * 12 / M$$

where C = the number of crimes reported and M = the number of months for which crime data were reported. For example, if an agency reported 70 homicides in 7 months, the data were imputed by multiplying 70 times $12/7 = 70*1.7143 = 120$ homicides. In all but 3 cases where values were imputed, a minimum of 6 months of actual data were available. For the 3 exceptions, 5 months of data were available.

If less than 5 months of data were available or if no data were reported in a given year, data from an adjacent year was substituted (a subsequent year was used first if available, or a prior year if not available). If data from an adjacent year was not available, the next adjacent year was utilized. In the *rare* case that data from the next adjacent year was not available, an average of two "third" adjacent years was used. To clarify using 1990 as an example for a missing data case, a value from 1991 was substituted, but if unavailable a 1989 value was used. If values were not available in either 1989 or 1991, a 1992 value was used. If 1992 data were unavailable, 1988 data were used. If neither 1988 nor 1992 data were available, the average of 1987 and 1993 was used.

Data from the 1990 Census are used in the analysis because they are most proximate in time to the four waves of LEMAS data and because Census 2000 data were not available at the time of data collection and preparation. The social, demographic and economic and data, therefore, are constant over time for each observation.[27]

OPERATIONALIZATION OF VARIABLES

This section includes the variable names, their description, operationalization, and source. Variable names that are different than descriptor names are in parentheses.

POLICE HOMICIDES (HOMICIDES): Three-year counts (sums) of incidents in which sworn municipal police officers with full arrest powers were murdered while acting in an official capacity around the years 1987, 1990, 1993 and 1996, LEOKA.

DIVORCED/SEPARATED (DIVORCED): The percentage of the population divorced or separated; (the number of divorced or separated males and females/number of males and females 15 years old and over) x 100, Bureau of the Census.

FAMILY DISRUPTION (FHHKIDS): Percentage of female-headed households with related children; (number of female-headed households with related children 18 years old and younger/total number of households) x 100, Bureau of the Census.

RESIDENTIAL STABILITY (RSTABILITY): Percentage of the population in same residence as in 1985; (the number of persons aged 5 and older residing in same home as five years ago/total persons aged 5 and older) x 100, Bureau of the Census.

RACIAL HETEROGENEITY (BLACK): The percentage of the population that is non-Hispanic black; (number of persons in the resident population that are non-Hispanic black/total resident population) x 100, Bureau of the Census.

BLACK RESIDENTIAL SEGREGATION (SEGREGATION): The *index of dissimilarity* or the degree to which two or more groups live separately from one another, i.e., the degree of unevenness in the distribution of black residents relative to white residents across census tracts in cities (Massey and Denton, 1988). The formula, from Sorensen, Taeuber, and Hollingsworth (1975), is

$$D = .5 * \sum \left| \frac{N_i}{N} - \frac{W_i}{W} \right|$$

Where i = city census tract;
N_i = number of black households in tract i;
$N = \sum N_i$ = total number of black households in city;
W_i = number of white households in tract i;
$W = \sum W_i$ = total number of white households in city.

The index reaches a value of 0 if black and white households are distributed equally among census tracts (no segregation) and a value of 1 if no tract has both white and black households (complete segregation). The index can be interpreted as the proportion of the minority population that would have to change residence to achieve an even distribution or zero degree of segregation (Massey and Denton, 1988:284; Sorensen, Taeuber, and Hollingsworth, 1975:126). Source: David Armstrong, Department of Sociology, The University at Albany, and Karen Parker, Center for Studies in Criminology and Law, University of Florida.
POPULATION DENSITY (DENSITY): The number of residents per square mile (total resident population/land area in square miles), Bureau of the Census.

POPULATION SIZE (POPULATION): The total number of city residents, Bureau of the Census.

POVERTY: Percentage of persons living below the official poverty level; (number of persons living below the poverty level/total number of persons) x 100, Bureau of the Census.

INCOME INEQUALITY (GINI): The Gini index[28] of household income inequality, calculated for N elements sorted from poorest to richest:

$$Gini = \sum_{i=1}^{N} 2(X_i - Y_i)\Delta X_i$$

where $X_i = 1/N$, Y_i = cumulative percentage of income by unit, and $\Delta X_i = X_i - X_{i-1}$, Bureau of the Census.

MEDIAN HOUSEHOLD INCOME (INCOME): Median household income, Bureau of the Census.

UNEMPLOYMENT: Percentage unemployed; (number unemployed in civilian labor force/number in civilian labor force) x 100, Bureau of the Census.

YOUNG MALES (MALES15-29): The percentage of males aged 15 – 29; (number of male residents aged 15 – 29 / the total number of residents) x 100, Bureau of the Census.

SOUTH: Unit location in the South; a dummy variable coded 1 if an agency is located in the South and 0 otherwise (Bureau of the Census classification).

CRIME: The sum of the number of Part I offenses known to the police, excluding arson (murder and nonnegligent manslaughter, forcible rape, robbery, aggravated assault, burglary, larceny-theft, and motor vehicle theft), UCR.

ARRESTS: The number of persons arrested for Part I offenses, excluding arson (murder and nonnegligent manslaughter, forcible rape, robbery, aggravated assault, burglary, larceny-theft, and motor vehicle theft), UCR.

FOOT PATROL (FOOT): Percentage of officers assigned to foot patrol; (the sum of the total number of officers assigned to foot patrol on shifts of 7 hours or longer for the 24-hour days of Wednesday and Saturday during the most recent week available with normal patrol activity / the total assigned to foot and non-foot patrol activities) x 100, LEMAS.

MANDATORY VEST WEAR POLICY (VEST): Departmental policy requiring patrol officers to wear body armor while on duty; a dummy variable coded 1 if an agency requires all field/patrol officers to wear body armor and zero otherwise, LEMAS.

NUMBER OF FIELD OFFICERS (FIELD): Number of officers assigned to field duty, LEMAS.

ONE-OFFICER PATROL UNITS (UNIT1): Percentage of one-officer patrol units; (the total number of police officers assigned to one-officer units on shifts of 7 hours or longer for the 24-hour days of Wednesday and Saturday during the most recent week available with normal patrol activity / the total number of one and two-officer units) x 100, LEMAS.

ACADEMY TRAINING (ACADEMY): Total amount of training; sum of the number of hours of field and classroom training required for new recruits, LEMAS.

CHEMICAL AGENTS (CHEM): Agency authorization of personal-issue chemical agents such as CS/CN and/or oleoresin capsicum; a dummy variable coded 1 if an agency authorizes chemical agents to its regular field/patrol officers and zero if it does not, LEMAS.

SEMIAUTOMATIC SIDEARMS (SEMIAUTO): Issuance or authorization of only semiautomatic sidearms; a dummy variable coded 1 if an agency supplies or authorizes *only* semi-automatic sidearms to its regular field/patrol officers and 0 if it supplies or authorizes revolvers only or revolvers and semi-automatic sidearms, LEMAS.

EDUCATIONAL REQUIREMENT (COLLEGE): Departmental educational requirement; a dummy variable coded 1 if agencies require new officer recruits to have at least some college and 0 otherwise, LEMAS.

SWORN FEMALES (FEMALE): Percentage of female police officers; (the number of full-time female sworn personnel / the total number of sworn personnel) x 100, LEMAS.

Table 3.1: Decision Rules for Dichotomous Variables

Original Data				Recoded Data			
'90	'93	'97		'90	'93	'97	Logic
0	0	.	=	Unchanged			Unknown if policy adopted in '97
0	.	.	=	Unchanged			Unknown if policy adopted in '93 or '97
0	.	0	=	0	0	0	Policy unlikely to change in '93
.	0	0	=	0	0	0	If no policy in '93 policy unlikely in '90
.	.	0	=	0	0	0	If no policy in '97 policy unlikely in '93 and '90
.	0	.	=	0	0	.	If no policy in '93 policy unlikely in '90, but '97 unknown
1	1	.	=	1	1	1	If policy in '93 policy likely in '97
1	.	.	=	1	1	1	If policy in '90 policy likely in '93 & '97
1	.	1	=	1	1	1	If policy in '90 & '97 policy likely in '93
.	1	1	=	Unchanged			Unknown if policy adopted in '90
.	.	1	=	Unchanged			Unknown if policy adopted in '90 or '93
.	1	.	=	.	1	1	If policy in 93 policy likely in '97, but unknown in '90

Note: Periods indicate missing data; 1 = policy present; 0 = policy absent

CHAPTER 4

Method and Analysis

This chapter begins with a description of the distributions of the variables used in the analysis. A preliminary assessment of the relationship of each regressor to the dependent variable is then made by estimating a series of bivariate regression models. This is followed by principal components analysis to reduce the large number of structural regressors into smaller numbers of interpretable factors, and the estimation of cross-section regression models for each wave of data. Finally, the four waves of data are pooled to improve precision of the estimates. These panel data are analyzed using generalized estimating equations, which are appropriate for data that are clustered (observations are correlated) and non-normally distributed (Liang and Zeger, 1986; Zeger and Liang, 1986).

DESCRIPTIVE STATISTICS

Descriptive statistics for the dependent variable (HOMICIDES) are provided in Table 5.1. Because the homicide incident counts are so low and exhibit large annual fluctuations, three-year counts (sums) are calculated around the years 1987, 1990, 1993, and 1996. For the full period (1986 – 1996), 239 officers were killed in 233 incidents. The general pattern across the 190 agencies is a decrease in the mean and number of police killed over the period of the analysis. Sixty-eight officers were murdered during 1986 – 1988 (mean = .36), whereas 50 were murdered during 1995 – 1997 (mean = .26). There is also a decrease in the *maximum* number of victim officers within any one agency over time, from nine officers murdered during 1986 – 1988 to four during 1995 – 1997.

Table 4.2 presents the descriptive statistics for the policing-related regressors obtained from LEMAS and the UCR (arrests). Additional details regarding the regressors beyond that provided in the operationalization section are provided in footnotes.

The percentage of the force assigned to one-officer units (UNIT1) was available for 1993 and 1997 only. This variable shows substantial cross-agency variability. In 1997, for example, the minimum and maximum percentages of the patrol force assigned to one-officer units are 9.5 and 100.0, respectively. Agencies tend to assign most officers to one-officer units, however, as indicated by means of approximately 86.0 in both years.

The percentage of the patrol force assigned to foot patrol (FOOT) also is available only for the years 1993 and 1997. Again, there is substantial variability, with minimum and maximum values of zero and over 50 percent, respectively, in both years. However, most agencies assign relatively few officers to foot patrol, as indicated by means of about 5.0.

The variable SEMIAUTO is an indicator of whether agencies supply *only* semiautomatic sidearms to its officers, or if the agency does not supply sidearms, whether it authorizes *only* semiautomatic sidearms.[29] The data show an increasing trend in the issuing or authorization only of semiautomatic sidearms to its regular field/patrol officers, with about three-fourths of agencies providing or authorizing only semiautomatics in 1997.

Information on whether or not agencies required all of their field officers to wear protective body armor (VEST) is available for 1990, 1993 and 1997 only. These data show an increasing trend in the percentage of agencies initiating mandatory vest-wear policies, ranging from 19 percent in 1990 to 42 percent in 1997.[30]

LEMAS collected information on the authorization of chemical agents beginning in 1990. In that year, agencies were asked whether they authorized the use of "chemical agents" such as "tear gas or mace" for patrol or field operations. In 1993 and 1997, oleoresin capsicum or "pepper spray" was included as an additional category. Thus, the variable CHEM_90 includes pepper spray as well as the older chemical agents mace and tear gas, whereas CHEM_93 and CHEM_97 indicate whether pepper spray was authorized for use by field and patrol officers. Seventy-five percent of agencies authorized the use of any type of chemical agent in 1990, 76 percent authorized the use of pepper spray in 1993, and 92 percent of agencies authorized it by 1997.

Over the four waves of data, the minimum number of full-time sworn field officers (FIELD) was 95 and the maximum was 33,513. The counts and averages show a general increase in the numbers of police employed over time.

The percentage of sworn officers that are women (FEMALE) varies substantially across time and over agencies. The minimum and maximum values over the four waves are 1 percent in 1987 and 29.3 percent in 1997, respectively. The mean values, while showing an increase in the proportion of females hired, indicate that most agencies employ relatively few female officers—on the average about 10 percent.

Although there is an increasing trend over the period, the majority of agencies do not require recruits to have any college education (COLLEGE). The percentage of agencies requiring some college education ranges from a low of 10 percent in 1987 to a high of 28 percent in 1997.

The variable ACADEMY indicates the sum of the total hours of classroom and field training required for new recruits. The data show substantial variability in total training time, ranging from a minimum of 176 hours in 1993 to a maximum 3,440 hours in 1987. The data also show a general decline over the period in the minimum and maximum values, though the minimum number increases from 1993 to 1997. The averages show a somewhat erratic pattern, increasing from 1987 to 1990, decreasing slightly between 1990 and 1993, and then increasing from 1993 to 1997.

The mean number of persons arrested for Part I crimes (ARRESTS) increased from 1987 to 1990, but then declined through 1997. These data show substantial variation within any one year; for instance, the number of arrests in 1990 ranged from 617 to 112,934.

Table 4.3 presents the descriptive statistics for the ecological factors. Most of the variables show substantial variation across cities. The 1990 residential population (POPULATION) ranges from just over 100,000 persons to over 7 million, and population density (DENSITY) ranges from 133 to 23,706 persons per square mile. Approximately one-third of the cities are located in the South (SOUTH). There are two measures of family disruption; the percentage of female-headed households with related children (FHHKIDS) ranges from 3.5 percent to 31.7 percent, and the percentage of the population divorced or separated (DIVORCED) ranges from 6.5 to 18.6 percent.

Regarding the economic variables, median household income (INCOME) ranges from a low of $16,925 to a high of $56,307, while the Gini index of income inequality (GINI) ranges from .33 to .57. The percentage of the persons living below the poverty level in 1989 (POVERTY) ranges from 2.6 to 37.3, and the percentage of the civilian labor force unemployed (UNEMPLOYMENT) ranges from 2.8 to 19.7.

Two regressors are race related. The racial dissimilarity index (SEGREGATION), a measure of black racial segregation in 1990, ranges from .14 to .88, while the percentage of the 1990 population that is non-Hispanic black ranges from .03 percent to 80.1 percent.

Residential stability (RSTABILITY) indicates that a low of 30.7 percent to a high of 67.2 percent of residents in 1990 resided in the same house as in 1985.

To control for the age and sex composition of cities, a combined variable indicating the percentage of the male population aged 15-29 was created (MALE15-29). This variable ranges from a low of 9.0 percent to a high of 22.1 percent. The pattern of the number of Part I offenses known to police (CRIME) follows that of arrests; they increase from 1987 to 1990, and decline thereafter. There is substantial variation in the number of offenses known across cities, ranging, for example, from a low of 3,334 to a high of 710,228 in 1990.

BIVARIATE POISSON REGRESSION ANALYSES

Determining the appropriate modeling procedure for analyzing the dependent variable requires an examination of its distribution. It is evident in Figure 4.1 that police homicides are characterized by a preponderance of zeros in each wave. The number of departments that experienced no homicides during the study period ranged from 150 (79%) to 156 (82%). The distributions are further characterized by small nonzero values and are not nearly normally distributed.

Figure 4.1: Distribution of Dependent Variable

A. N Incidents Officers Murdered, 1986 – 1988

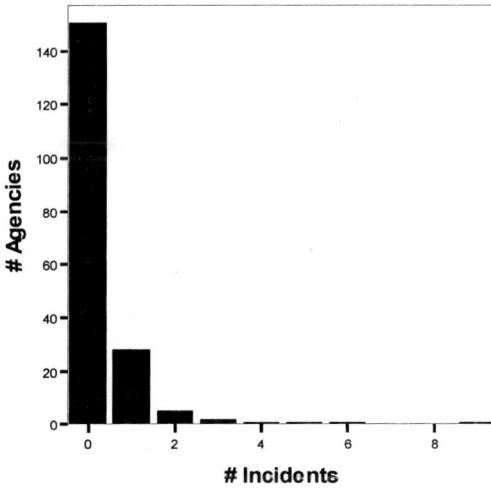

B. N Incidents Officers Murdered, 1989 – 1991

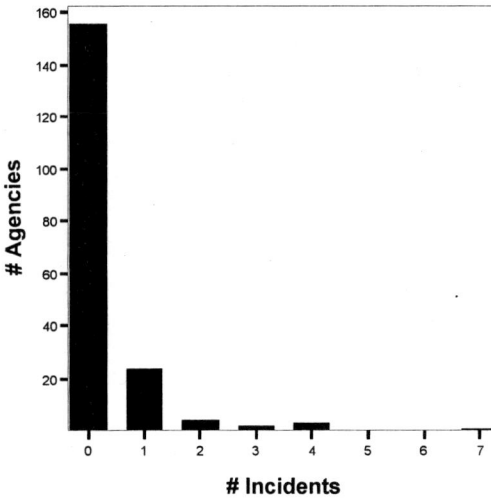

Figure 4.1 (continued) Distribution of Dependent Variable

C. N Incidents Officers Murdered, 1992 – 1994

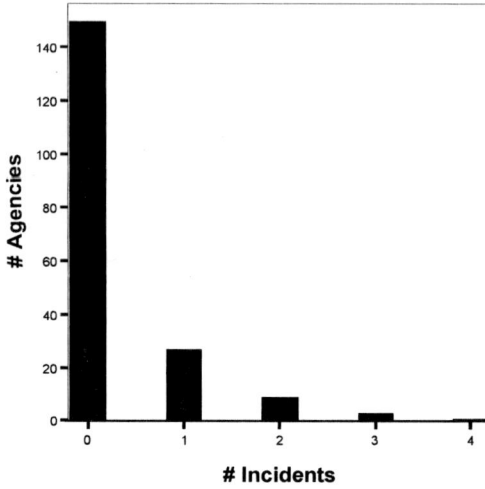

D. N Incidents Officers Murdered, 1995 – 1997

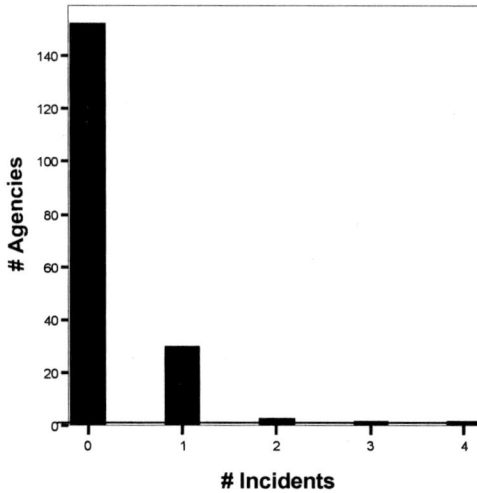

Being semi-continuous, the standard linear regression model might suffice if the mean of the outcome was large (Cameron and Trivedi 1998:2), but when it is small (only .26 to .36 in this study), application of the linear model can produce biased, inefficient, and inconsistent estimates (Long 1997:217).

Two common analytic strategies are to transform the dependent variable to approximate normality and proceed with linear regression, or to combine all outcomes greater than zero into a single category and employ binary logistic regression. Mathematical transformations of these data, however, are unable to approximate a normal distribution, and dichotomizing the dependent variable for use with binary logistic regression is undesirable because it results in a loss of efficiency (Cameron and Trivedi 1998:86). Instead, Poisson regression, appropriate for outcomes with many zeros and large positive skew, is used as the starting point for the regression analysis (Cameron and Trivedi, 1998:59-70; Long, 1997:217-229).

Table 4.4 presents the results of the bivariate Poisson regression analyses. For each wave of data, the exponentiated coefficients (incidence rate ratios),[31] significance levels, and pseudo-R^2 values for each regressor are given. Policing variables are listed first, followed by the ecological correlates.[32]

Consistent with expectations, the number of arrests for Part I crimes, and the percentage of officers on foot patrol are significantly and positively associated with the number of homicides in each wave. As indicators of exposure, these results suggest the greater the percentage of officers on a force assigned to foot patrol and the more arrests police make, the more visible and accessible they are to the public and motivated offenders, thereby increasing opportunities for their victimization.

The number of sworn officers assigned to field duties is, as expected, also significantly and positively associated with risk of officer homicide in each wave. This variable, used as one measure of proximity to motivated offenders, suggests that higher field officer density increases opportunities for homicides of police.

The percentage of one-officer units and mandatory vest-wear policies, entered as measures of guardianship, are statistically significant in each wave but are in the opposite direction hypothesized. Although the relationships may change in the multivariate models, it may be that departments where the risk of officer homicide is low tend to have fewer officers assigned to two-officer units, and agencies in cities where the risk of homicide is high may be more likely to have mandatory vest-wear policies.

Most of the remaining policing regressors appear to be unrelated to homicides of police or have inconsistent effects. The issuance or authorization of only semiautomatic sidearms is statistically insignificant in each wave even at the .10 level, though it is in the expected direction in three of four waves. Authorization of chemical agents is significant only at the .10 level in 1990; it is positive in 1990 and 1993, but inversely related in 1997. The total amount of training (ACADEMY) is significant at the .05 level only in 1993, and the direction of its effect changes year-to-year. The educational requirement variable (COLLEGE) is significant only at the .10 level in 1987, and also changes direction across waves. Surprisingly, the percentage of sworn female officers is highly significant and positive in each wave.

Of the policing regressors, the number of field officers (proximity) and arrests (exposure) generally explain the most "variance" in the outcome (pseudo-R^2 values range from .11 to .26), followed in magnitude by the percentage of sworn females (.08 to .09); the remaining regressors explain smaller amounts of variation in police homicides.

Among the structural and crime regressors, population size and density are highly significant and in the expected direction in all waves, suggesting that large and dense populations are associated with increased opportunities for the victimization of officers. The family instability variables (divorced/separated, female-headed households with own children) are significant at or below the .05 level in most years, except that in 1993 DIVORCED is significant only at the .10 level. The race-based regressors, percentage black and black racial segregation, are highly significant and in the expected direction in all waves. Three of the four economic variables are highly significant and in the expected direction in each wave (POVERTY, GINI,[33] UNEMPLOYMENT); the impact of income is in the expected direction in all waves, but it is statistically insignificant in 1987. Location in the South is significant only at the .10 level and only in 1993. Residential stability is highly significant in each wave, but it is positive, which is opposite the expected direction. The percentage of young males in the population is statistically significant in one wave only and is inversely associated with the outcome in all waves, and thus also opposite the direction hypothesized. Finally, the number of Part I offenses known is highly significant and in the expected direction in each wave.

The ecological regressors explaining relatively large amounts of variation in the outcome are crime (14-27%), population size (11-23%), black racial segregation (11-18%), population density (7-14%), and percentage black (4-11%).

To summarize, the bivariate regressions show that most regressors are significant and in the expected direction. Police employed in departments characterized by higher levels of officer *exposure* (percent assigned to foot patrol and number of arrests) appear to be at greater risk for homicide. Measures of guardianship, however, are either statistically unrelated to homicides of police in bivariate regressions (SEMIAUTO, CHEM, ACADEMY), or the direction of the effects are most often opposite that hypothesized (UNIT1, VEST).

Most indicators of *proximity* to motivated offenders appear to be related to homicides of police (field officer density, population size and density, family instability, adverse economic conditions, percentage black, racial segregation, and crime), though the effect of residential stability is opposite that expected. Regressors nonsignificant in most waves are the percentage of young males in the population and unit location in the South.

PRINCIPAL COMPONENTS ANALYSIS

Including 24 independent variables in a regression model raises concerns not only about multiple comparisons (i.e., the probability of finding a significant relationship by chance alone), but multicollinearity as well. Many regressors are similar conceptually, and it is expected that several will be highly collinear, making it difficult to assess their independent effects. An examination of the correlation matrices for each wave of the data shows this to be the case (not shown). For instance, correlations among median household income, percent below poverty, percent unemployed, percent black and percent female-headed households with children correlate between .75 and .82 (absolute values). Of greater concern are population size, the number of sworn field officers, crimes known, and arrests, which correlate, for example, between .91 and .97 in 1990.

Tests for collinearity using multiple linear regression confirm the presence of severe multicollinearity (see Table A2 in the Appendix). As an example, entering all the 1997 policing, crime, and structural regressors produced variance inflation factors ranging from 13.5 to 47.8 for five regressors (values greater than 10 are indicative of collinearity problems) and 13 condition indices ranging from 16.1 to over 170 (values greater than 15 indicate a possible problem, while values greater than 30 suggest a serious problem).

Because of concerns regarding the negative impacts of multicollinearity on the regression estimates (Land, McCall, and Cohen, 1990), principal components analysis is used to linearly transform sets of correlated structural variables into smaller groups of uncorrelated components. Based on research by Wilson (1987), Massey and Denton (1988), Sampson, Morenoff, and Earls (1999), Sampson, Raudenbush, and Earls (1997), and other ecological studies on homicide and violence using data reduction procedures (Baller, Anslen, Messner, Deane, and Hawkins, 2001; Land, McCall, and Cohen, 1990; Lauritsen, 2001; Parker, 2001, Parker and McCall, 1999), the principal components analysis is expected to produce at least two components. One is expected to be indicative of "concentrated disadvantage", consisting roughly of indicators of poor economic conditions, family disruption, residential mobility, and large and isolated black populations.

A second expected component normally would be population structure (population size and density). However, population size was excluded from the principal components analysis because it is used later to modify the field officer density variable (number of field officers). This was necessary because of very high first-order correlations between the number of field officers and arrests (discussed later). The modified officer density variable is calculated as the number of field officers per 10,000 population, and is only moderately correlated with arrests. Excluding population size from the principal components analysis had no impact on the obtained solution, other than that population density is a lone factor (both loaded together when included).

The abbreviated rotated principal components matrix is presented in Table 4.5 (see the Appendix, Table A3, for the full output). Explaining 74.1 percent of the variance overall, the principal components solution appears reasonable and interpretable, and is largely consistent with theory and empirical results obtained in previous ecological studies of homicide and violence (Baller et al., 2001; Land, McCall, and Cohen, 1990; Lauritsen, 2001; Massey and

Denton, 1988; Parker, 2001, Parker and McCall, 1999; Sampson, Morenoff, and Earls, 1999; Sampson, Raudenbush, and Earls, 1997; Wilson, 1987).

As anticipated, component one indicates that cities characterized by economic disadvantage (high levels of poverty, income inequality, unemployment, and low income) also tend to have high levels of family disruption (divorce, female-headed households), and large and isolated black populations. All loadings on this component are above .5, and the component overall explains 48.6 percent of the variance. Component one is referred to as *resource deprivation* (DEPRIVATION).

Component two loads on two regressors (inversely related); these are the percentage of the population still residing in the same house as in 1985 and the percentage of young males. Explaining 13.2 percent of the variance, this component is called *residential stability* (STABILITY).

Component three refers to population structure, though as discussed, it consists only of population density (DENSITY). It explains 12.3 percent of the variance.

Table 4.6 shows the results of regressing police homicides on the components in bivariate regressions. Each component is statistically significant at the .05 level in each wave. DEPRIVATION and DENSITY are positive and in the hypothesized directions, but STABILITY is also positive, and therefore opposite the direction anticipated (possible reasons for this are explored later).

MULTIPLE POISSON REGRESSION ANALYSIS

A major goal of this research is to test whether the addition of opportunity factors measured at the organizational level (guardianship and exposure) contribute to an explanation of homicides of police net of structural conditions (proximity to motivated offenders). Therefore, the multivariate regression analysis begins with the estimation of a series of cross-sectional submodels. The first examines whether indicators of guardianship are associated with homicides of police; a second submodel tests the effects of exposure, and a third examines the impacts of proximity (criminogenic structural conditions). Models are then combined sequentially, starting with proximity as a base and then adding exposure and guardianship variables. Finally, a model is estimated with all regressors simultaneously (including control variables). Following the cross-sectional analyses, a panel regression model using generalized estimating equations (GEE) is estimated.

Guardianship

Table 4.7 presents the results of regressing police homicides on the *guardianship* variables for the four waves of data. Exponentiated coefficients or incidence rate ratios (IRR), significance levels, likelihood ratios (LL), likelihood ratio chi-square tests of the fit of the estimated models versus a naive or constants-only model (LRχ2), the Poisson goodness-of-fit test (Poisgof), and McFadden's pseudo-R^2 values are provided.

The results show that the percentage of police assigned to one-officer patrol units (UNIT1) is significantly associated with homicides of police in 1997 and 1993 (the only two years for which this variable is available), but as in the bivariate models the direction of the effect is opposite that hypothesized. In 1997, for example, each percentage increase in the number of police assigned to one-officer units is associated with a two percent *decrease* in the expected number of police homicides (e^β = .9803). The impact of mandatory vest-wear policies (VEST) is significant in each of the three years for which this variable is available, though only at the .10 level in 1997 (p = .087). Its effects are also opposite that expected; in 1993, for instance, having a mandatory vest-wear policy is associated with a 78 percent *increase* in the expected number of homicides. The effect of the authorization of chemical agents for all line officers (CHEM) is significant only in 1990 (p = .052), and it is positive in 1990 and 1993 and negative in 1997. The issuing or authorizing of semiautomatic sidearms only (SEMIAUTO) and the amount of academy and field training (ACADEMY) are statistically unrelated to homicides of police in all four waves.

The Poisson goodness-of-fit tests (Poisgof) suggest the Poisson regression model is appropriate for these data. The likelihood ratio chi-square test statistics indicate the models for all years but 1987 fit better than a constants-only model. In 1987 neither regressor is significant even at the .10 level, and the LR test confirms they do not contribute to an explanation of homicides of police in that wave (p = .28). Finally, despite significant LR statistics for the 1990-1997 waves, the pseudo-R^2 values suggest that as a group these regressors explain little of the variation in homicides (only 4 to 6 percent).

Unexpectedly, the results suggest that rather than being associated with fewer homicides of police, the proportion of two-officer patrol units, mandatory vest-wear policies, and the authorization of pepper spray (in 1990) are associated with *increases* in homicide counts. It may be that the direction of these effects are a function of the static nature of the model. In other words, agencies located in particularly dangerous jurisdictions may initiate changes to reduce officer risk of homicide, such as requiring officers to wear protective vests and increasing the proportion of the patrol force assigned to two-officer units.

In summary, at this preliminary stage of the analysis the guardianship variables explain little of the variation in murders of police across departments and there is little evidence that they are associated with fewer police homicides.

Exposure

Table 4.8 presents the results for the two *exposure* variables. Unlike in the bivariate model, when arrests for Part I crimes are included the percentage of officers assigned to foot patrol (FOOT) is unrelated to homicides of police in 1993 and 1997, the two years for which this regressor is available. The number of arrests, however, is highly significant and in the hypothesized direction in all four waves of data. The results suggest that each additional 1,000 arrests is associated with a 3.7 to a 4.6 percent increase in the expected number of police homicides (assuming a linear relationship). The LR tests confirm the contribution of ARRESTS to each model, and the pseudo-R^2 values suggest this variable explains large amounts of the variation in homicides each year (from 14 to 25 percent). Again, the Poisson goodness-of-fit tests suggest the Poisson regression model is appropriate.

The results support the notion that arrests for serious offenses increase opportunities for the victimization of police by increasing officer exposure to motivated offenders. However, the argument that increases in the proportion of officers assigned to foot patrol increases risk of homicide because foot-patrol officers are more visible and accessible is not supported when arrests are included in the model.

Proximity

The results of regressing police homicides on the three factors derived from the principal components analysis, conceptualized as indicators of proximity to motivated offenders, are presented in Table 4.9.

Resource deprivation (DEPRIVATION) is highly significant and in the hypothesized direction in each model; each one-unit increase in this component is associated with a 56 to 90 percent increase in the expected number of homicides (assuming a linear relationship), depending on the year examined. Similarly, population density (DENSITY) is significant in each wave, and suggests the expected number of homicides increase from 35 to 67 percent with each unit increase in this component. The component residential stability (STABILITY) is statistically significant at the .05 level in 1997 and 1990 only, and the direction of the effect is positive and thus continues to be opposite that hypothesized.[34] In terms of overall fit, the LR tests indicate each model fits better than a constants-only model, and each explains a substantial amount of the variation in the outcome, (R^2 = .150 to .202). The Poisgof tests continue to suggest Poisson regression is appropriate for these data.

An alternative (or in addition) to using criminogenic conditions as a measure of proximity to motivated offenders is the number of Index offenses known to the police (CRIME), which may be considered a more direct and perhaps preferred measure of proximity (Miethe and Meier, 1994:47). When entered as a single regressor (Table 4.4), crimes known is highly significant in each year, and the amount of variance explained (13.7 to 27.4%) is greater than that explained by the three principal components in three of the waves and nearly equivalent to the amount explained in 1993 (14.5 vs. 13.7%). The important question is, however, whether the level of reported crime adds to the explanatory model net of the three principal components. The results after adding CRIME are shown in Table 4.10.

The effect of CRIME continues to be highly significant in each wave, ($p \leq .001$), and its impact is substantial. Across the four waves of data, each additional 10,000 crimes is associated with a 4.7 percent to 10.5 percent increase in the expected number of police homicides (assuming a linear relationship), net of the impact of the three principal components. As indicated by the pseudo-R^2 values, the amount of "explained variance" increases by 5.1 to 16.3 percent with the addition of CRIME. The impact of DEPRIVATION changes little with the addition of CRIME and it remains highly significant. However, except for STABILITY in 1997, STABILITY and DENSITY drop out of the model (using a .05 level of significance), suggesting population density and residential stability/young males are unrelated to homicides of police once reported levels of crime are controlled. Diagnostics indicate collinearity among the regressors is not a concern in these models (not shown).[35]

The next step in the model building process is to include the number of field officers as an additional measure of proximity. As noted earlier, it is assumed that proximity is a function of both the density of motivated offenders (measured by criminogenic conditions and the number of crimes known) plus the number of police officers assigned to field duties. Adding the number of field officers to the proximity model (not shown), however, proved to be problematic in that this variable is highly collinear with CRIME (first-order correlations range from .85 to .96). In addition, the number of field officers and ARRESTS (added to the model later) correlate almost perfectly in each wave of the data (.94 to .96).

Therefore, a new variable is created that remains consistent with the concept of field officer density but is relatively uncorrelated with the other regressors; this is the number of field officers per 10,000 population (FIELD2). First-order correlations between FIELD2 and CRIME are moderate (.34 to .51), and the correlations between FIELD2 and ARRESTS are substantially reduced (.37 to .47).

Table 4.11 presents the results after the addition of FIELD2 to the proximity model. FIELD2 is statistically significant at conventional levels in all four models, and holding constant the effects of the other regressors indicates that a 10-unit increase in field officer density is associated with a 37.6 to 112.9 percent increase in police homicides (assuming linearity). Generally, the magnitude and statistical significance of the other regressors decline after the addition of FIELD2, though most regressors that were significant in the models without FIELD2 remain significant in the models with it included. DEPRIVATION, though, while remaining significant in 1990 and 1993 at the .05 level, becomes borderline significant in 1997 ($p = .055$) and statistically insignificant at the .10 level in 1987 ($p = .558$). In addition, DENSITY, which was significant only at the .10 level in 1987 ($p = .074$) becomes highly significant following the introduction of FIELD2 ($p \leq .001$), and its impact increases substantially.

The reasons for these inconsistent effects are unclear. The problem does not appear to be due to multicollinearity among the regressors; linear regression models (not shown) produce variance inflation factors less than 2.05 and condition indices less than 9.21 in all waves. The principal components do not vary over time, but as shown earlier in Tables 4.2 and 4.3, the average number of field officers and reported crimes vary substantially over the period under study. Thus, the inconsistent effects may be due to complex interactions among the regressors. However, the addition of linear interaction terms to the 1987 model did not produce any significant effects at the .10 level (not shown).[36]

Despite certain inconsistencies in the models across waves, the overall evidence suggests that resource deprivation, the level of serious reported crime, and field officer density, conceptualized as measures of proximity to motivated offenders, increase substantially opportunities for homicides of police. All models fit better than a constants-only model, and compared with earlier models, each explains a somewhat greater amount of the variation in the outcome (R^2 = .21 to .35). The Poisson goodness-of-fit tests continue to indicate the Poisson regression model is appropriate for the analysis.

Retaining CRIME in the model is problematic, however, when exposure factors are added. This is because ARRESTS and CRIME are highly correlated (first-order correlations range from .93 to .98), and estimating the proximity model including ARRESTS using linear regression (not shown) suggests a serious problem with multicollinearity. Although condition indices were only moderately high (ranging from 10.35 to 13.84), variance inflation factors for ARRESTS and CRIME were greater than 21.00 in 1987, 1990, and 1993 (they were between 8.03 and 8.16 in 1997). This suggests that both regressors should not be included in the same model.

Since the focus of this research is on examining the influence of police organizational factors on risk of officer homicide, the choice is to include ARRESTS rather than CRIME. Although there is little distinction between these regressors empirically, conceptually arrests reflect more closely the behavior of police (Wilson, 1975) than does reported crime, which presumably reflects "true" levels of crime plus the reporting behavior of the community (Schneider and Wiersema, 1990). This choice allows retention of the remaining indicators of proximity, which are consistent with measures used in much prior research on opportunity factors (Hough, 1987; Miethe and McDowall, 1993; Miethe and Meier, 1994; Sampson and Wooldredge, 1987).

Combined Models: Adding Exposure

Regressors most commonly used in prior research on homicides of police have been structural indicators of criminogenic conditions (see Table 3.1), and of the research questions posed, a major one is whether other factors, such as guardianship and exposure, affect risk of homicide net of criminogenic conditions. Accordingly, the next step in the analysis is to add sequentially exposure and guardianship factors to the proximity model. Indicators of exposure—the percentage of the force assigned to foot patrol (FOOT) and the number of Index crime arrests (ARRESTS)—are added first. These results are presented in Table 4.12 (Panels A–D).

The output is organized in the following manner; starting with 1997, submodels for each wave of data are presented in the separate panels. To ease comparisons, Model 1 in each panel repeats the results for the *proximity* model. Model 2 in each panel shows the results after adding the *exposure* variables ARRESTS and FIELD2. Model 3 adds the *guardianship* variables to this model, and Model 4 adds the *control* variables to Model 3 (percent sworn female officers, unit location in the South, and educational requirements).

As shown in Model 2 for all waves (Panels A–D), adding the exposure variables has little impact on the size and significance levels of the proximity-related variables. The exception is population density (DENSITY), which reverses direction in 1997, 1990, and 1987. Further, though DENSITY is highly significant in 1993, 1990, and 1987 in Model 1, it becomes insignificant in 1993 ($p = .212$) and 1990 ($p = .146$) with the addition of the exposure variables. Although the reason for the inconsistent effects of DENSITY across waves is not clear, the sign reversals in three of the waves suggest ARRESTS and DENSTY are somehow related (this is explored later).[37]

The percentage of the force assigned to foot patrol (FOOT) is insignificant in 1997 ($p = .765$); it is nearly significant at the .05 level in 1993 ($p = .069$), but opposite the direction hypothesized. ARRESTS, though, continues to be highly significant and positive in all waves when added to the proximity model. This suggests that more arrests are associated with increases in officer risk of homicide net of criminogenic conditions.

Combined Models: Adding Guardianship

Model 3 adds to Model 2 the percentage of the force assigned to one-officer patrols (UNIT1), whether agencies issue or authorize only semiautomatic sidearms to their officers (SEMIAUTO), have a mandatory vest-wear policy for all line officers (VEST), whether they authorize chemical agents for line officers (CHEM), and the total number of academy and field training hours required for new recruits (ACADEMY).

None of the guardianship regressors are statistically significant at the .05 level in any wave when proximity and exposure factors are in the model. ACADEMY is significant at the .10 level only in 1990 ($p = .099$). The direction of its effect in 1990 (and also in 1993) is consistent with the notion that more training reduces the risk of officer homicide, but because its effect is inconsistent across waves and not significant at the conventional level, the tentative conclusion is that it is unrelated to homicides of police. To check further for the potential contribution of these regressors, each was successively entered and removed from Model 2 (results not shown). None, however, were significant at the .10 level.[38]

There are no substantial impacts on the estimates and significance levels of FIELD2 with the addition of the guardianship regressors. DEPRIVATION, however, becomes statistically insignificant at the .05 level in 1997 ($p = .162$), though it remains significant in 1993 and 1990 and is unchanged in 1987 (remains insignificant). DENSITY also changes little in most waves, though it becomes nearly significant at the .05 level in 1990 ($p = .065$). STABILITY remains significant and changes little in magnitude in 1997, and it continues to be statistically insignificant in the remaining waves.

Table 4.13 presents a summary of the statistically significant findings across waves. Regressors significant at the .05 level are represented by single asterisks and directional signs; regressors significant at the .10 level are indicated by directional signs only, and "na" indicates variables not available in waves. As the table shows, homicides of police are consistently related to the number of field officers per 10,000 population (FIELD2) and the number of arrests for Part I crimes (ARRESTS). The effect of DEPRIVATION is in the expected direction, but it is significant at the .05 level in two waves only (1993 and 1990). STABILITY and DENSITY are related inconsistently to the outcome, each being significant at the .05 level in only one wave.

Based on the results so far, the tentative conclusion is that cross-agency variation in the guardianship factors has no impact on officer risk of homicide. Rather, the risk appears to be associated most consistently with proximity to motivated offenders—measured by the density of field officers (and possibly resource deprivation)—and exposure, as measured by the number of arrests for serious crime.

A final note regarding these results; observe that the pseudo R^2 value *decreases* with the addition of the guardianship variables in 1987 (compare Models 2 and 3). This is because information on SEMIAUTO is missing for the New York City Police Department in that year. If SEMIAUTO is excluded from Model 4, the R^2 value increases from .281 to .344 (results not shown). This increase in R^2 when New York City is included suggests an improvement in the fit of the model. Because the exclusion of observations due to missing data on certain regressors may adversely impact the analysis, trimmed models are considered later.

Combined Models: Adding Control Variables

Added to Model 3 are the control variables percentage of female sworn officers (FEMALE), unit location in the South (SOUTH), and the percentage of departments requiring at least some college (COLLEGE). These results are presented in Model 4. A comparison of Model 4 to Model 3 for 1997 shows little change in the results with the addition of the control variables, and none of the control variables are statistically significant at the .10 level in 1997.

In 1993, DEPRIVATION and FIELD2, both significant at the .05 level in Model 3, become statistically insignificant at the .10 level ($p = .198$ and .189, respectively) once controls are added. Surprisingly, two regressors become significant at the .05 or .10 level with the addition of the control variables. Specifically, DENSITY becomes significant at the .05 level ($p = .025$) and its coefficient increases in magnitude from 1.21 to 1.55, and although the magnitude of the coefficient for FOOT changes little with the addition of controls, it becomes significant at the .10 level ($p = .069$). Among the control variables, only SOUTH is statistically significant at the .10 level ($p = .012$), suggesting that agency location in the South is associated with a 182 percent increase in the expected number of officer homicides in 1993.

In 1990, data on the percentage of the force assigned to foot patrol (FOOT) and the percentage assigned to one-officer patrol units (UNIT1) are unavailable. Among the available regressors, the most notable change following the addition of the control variables is that officer density (FIELD2), significant at the .05 level ($p = .039$) in Model 3 becomes statistically insignificant at the .10 level in Model 4 ($p = .123$). DENSITY, significant at the .10 level in Model 3 also becomes statistically insignificant in Model 4 ($p = .327$), as does ACADEMY ($p = .119$). DEPRIVATION decreases somewhat in magnitude, but remains statistically significant at the .05 level ($p = .034$). None of the control variables are significant at the .10 level in 1990.

In 1987, in addition to FOOT and UNIT1, information on mandatory vest-wear policies (VEST) and the authorization of chemical agents (CHEM) are not available. In this model, there is little change in the estimates and significance levels of the remaining regressors with the addition of the control variables. Among the controls, only the percentage of sworn female officers (FEMALE) is significant at the .10 level ($p = .027$).

Table 4.14 provides a summary of the findings from Model 4 across the four waves of data. Except for ARRESTS, the results are less consistent across the waves than in Model 3. FIELD2, significant in all four waves in Model 3, is significant in only two waves in Model 4 (1997 and 1987). DEPRIVATION is now significant only in 1990, whereas in Model 3 it was significant in 1990 and 1993. In Model 3, DENSITY was significant in 1990 ($p < .10$) and in 1987 ($p < .05$), and exhibited an inverse relationship with homicides. In Model 4, DENSITY retains its level of significance and direction in 1987, it becomes significant in 1993 ($p < .05$) but is *positive*, and it is no longer significant at the .10 level in 1990. ACADEMY, significant at the .10 level in 1990 in Model 3, drops out in Model 4. FOOT, however, insignificant in 1993 and 1997 in Model 3 becomes significant at the .10 level in Model 4 in 1993. The effect of STABILITY continues to be significant at the .05 level only in 1997.

Although the results shown in Model 3 vary somewhat with the addition of the control variables in Model 4, overall, the Poisson regression results continue to provide most support for exposure and proximity factors, primarily though the effects of field officer density (FIELD2) and arrests for Part I offenses (ARRESTS). Notably, none of the guardianship variables are significant in any wave at the .05 level.

Among the control variables, unit location in the South and the percentage of sworn female officers are significant at the .05 level, but only in one wave each.

REGRESSION DIAGNOSTICS

Given the large number of regressors in Model 4, it is reasonable to suspect collinearity among the regressors. Collinearity diagnostics (not shown) obtained using multiple linear regression show variance inflation factor values of only 2.42 and smaller across all four waves. However, the 1997 and 1993 models had components with condition indices of 29.71 and 24.46, respectively, suggesting a collinearity problem (condition indices for 1990 and 1987 were 15.21 or lower). An examination of the variance proportions in 1997 indicates this component accounts for 98 percent of the variance in the constant and 52 percent of the variance in the percentage of the force assigned to one-officer patrol units (UNIT1). In 1993, the values are 97 and 64 percent, respectively (UNIT1 is not available in 1990 and 1987).

To assess the impact of collinearity, Model 4 was reestimated without UNIT1. The results of the Poisson regression for 1997 (not shown) indicate virtually no changes in the estimates and significance levels after dropping this variable. In 1993, the major difference is that the significance level for FIELD2 drops from .069 to .053. Therefore, UNIT1 is retained, and an examination of residuals and influential cases is conducted next.

Residual and Influential Case Analyses

Panels A–D in Figure 4.2 show plots of deviance residuals against case observation numbers for each wave of data. In general, the residuals appear to be reasonably well behaved (i.e., no individual cases with large values that stand far out far from the group), with the larger, positive residuals the result of model underpredictions of homicides of police for those cases. The pattern of residuals for 1993 shows two cases that standout somewhat from the remainder; these are Oakland, CA (deviance = 2.63) and Winston-Salem, NC (deviance = 2.55). However, dropping these observations from the 1993 model did not change appreciably either the magnitude or significance levels of estimated coefficients (results not shown).

Figure 4.2: Deviance Residuals for Poisson Regressions

A. 1997

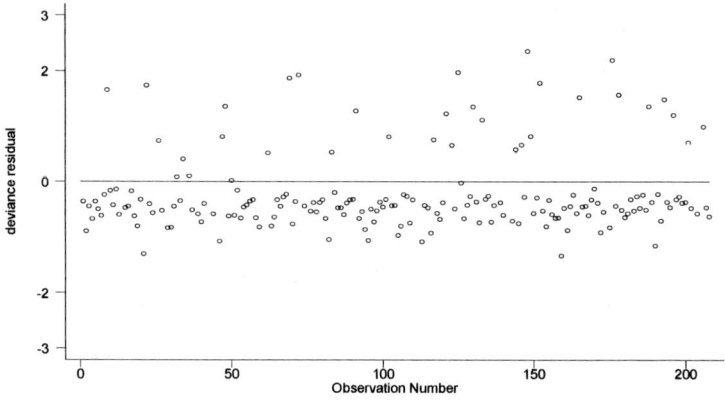

B. 1993

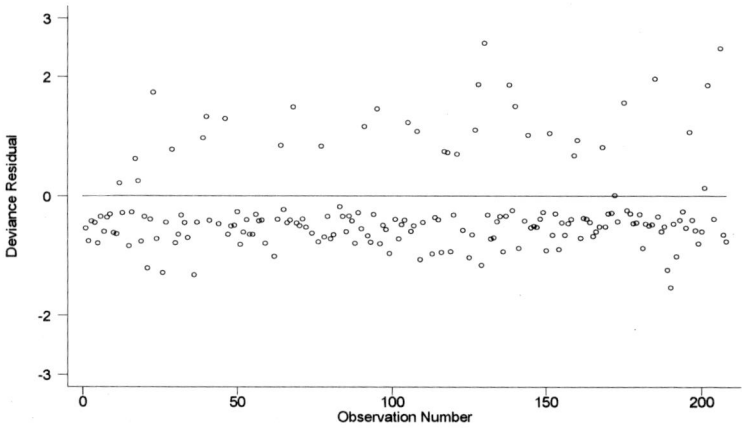

Figure 4.2 (continued) Deviance Residuals for Poisson Regressions

C. 1990

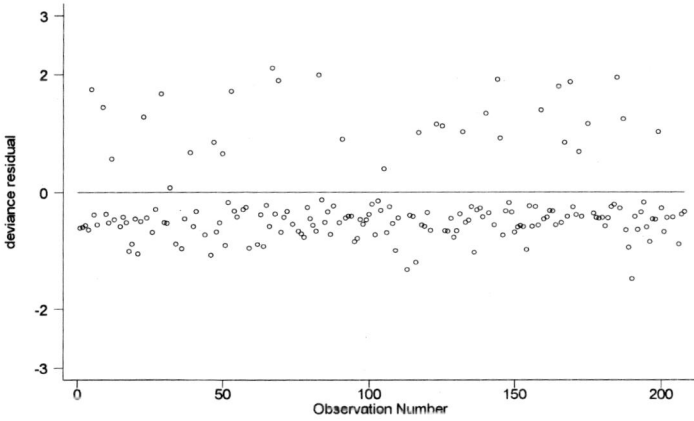

D. 1987

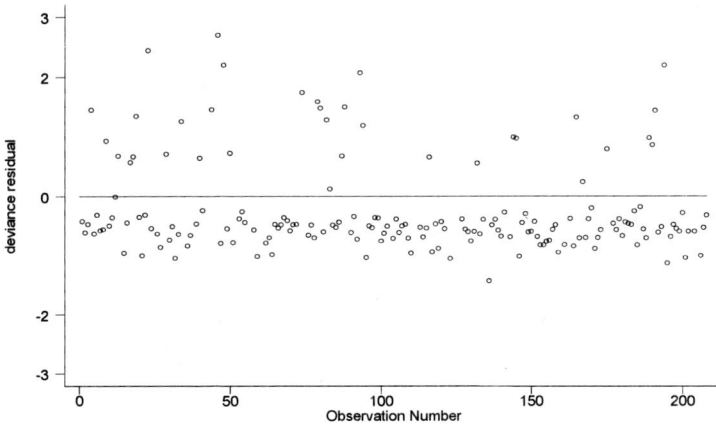

Although the patterns of residuals across the four waves show little cause for concern, it is still advisable to determine whether any observations have an undue influence on the obtained regression results. Diagonal entries from the regression models' hat matrices are useful for detecting influential observations (Cameron and Trivedi, 1998:150). Plots of the diagonal entries from the hat matrices, h_{ii}, against observation numbers are presented in Figure 5.3, Panels A–D. The symbols is these plots are weighted by their respective diagonal hat values.

Panels A–C in Figure 5.3 suggest New York City exerts the strongest influence on the regression results in 1997, 1993 and 1990 ($h = .88, .89.$ and $.90$, respectively). In 1987 (Panel D), Chicago exerts the greatest influence ($h = .69$), but this is because New York City is excluded due to missing data on the variable SEMIAUTO. If this regressor is excluded and the 1987 model reestimated, New York City is also the most influential case in that year ($h = .93$), followed by the District of Columbia ($h = .65$) and Detroit ($h = .53$).

The District of Columbia is the next most influential observation ($h = .63$ to $.77$), except in 1987, when Chicago is ($h = .69$). Generally, Chicago ($h = .54$ to $.69$) and Detroit ($h = .52$ to $.55$) display moderately high values in most waves, and Los Angeles does in 1987 ($h = .51$). However, when New York City is included by dropping SEMIAUTO from the model in 1987, the value of h for Chicago and Los Angeles decline to $.23$ and $.13$, respectively.

To assess the impact on the above observations on the regression results, they are dropped and the models reestimated (regression results not shown). A summary of the changes in the significance levels of variables after dropping the cases is provided in Table 4.15. Delta symbols (Δ) indicate changes in significance level, with Δ^{ns} indicating variables that are not significant at the .10 level but that *were* significant at the .05 level prior to dropping the influential observations. Delta symbols followed by *p*-values indicate regressors that were not significant, but *become* significant at the .05 or .10 level after dropping the influential observations. Changes in significance levels from .05 to .10 and vice versa are also indicated by *p*-values. Finally, asterisks followed by directional signs indicate regressors that remained statistically significant at the .05 level following the removal of influential cases.

Dropping the three influential observations in 1997 causes two regressors to become non-significant. The *p*-value for FIELD2 changes from .017 to .292, while for ARRESTS it changes from .033 to .150. The only other major change in the 1997 model is in the pseudo-R^2, which declines substantially from .273 to .154 suggesting a poorer fit.

Dropping the four observations in 1993 has only minor impacts on the regression results; the major difference is in the significance level for FOOT, which changes from .069 to .501. The R^2 also decreases somewhat, from .263 to .227.

In 1990, the significance level for DEPRIVATION changes from .034 to .412, whereas for SOUTH it changes from .145 to .026. The R^2 declines substantially from .371 to .252.

When observations are dropped in the 1987 model, the significance level for DENSITY changes from .050 to .100 and for FEMALE from .022 to .104. ACADEMY, however, changes from .125 to .052. The R2 decreases somewhat from .303 to .259.

Recall that the identification of influential cases in 1987 was conducted with New York City already excluded because of missing data on SEMIAUTO. Excluding SEMIAUTO from the regression model produces a different set of influential cases than when it is included (these are New York City, the District of Columbia, and Detroit). Excluding SEMIAUTO and dropping these observations influences only ACADEMY and FEMALE, causing the significance level of the former to change from .159 to .052, and the latter to change from .039 to .061. The R^2 decreases substantially from .363 to .283.

In summary, dropping the influential observations identified in Panels A–D in Figure 4.3 impacted the significance levels of several regressors. A comparison of Table 4.14 with Table 4.15 shows that DEPRIVATION, statistically significant at the .05 level in 1990, became insignificant with removal of the influential cases. DENSITY, significant at the .05 level in 1987 and 1997, remained significant in 1997 but not in 1987. ARRESTS, significant at the .05 level in all four waves, became insignificant in 1997. FIELD2 was significant at the .05 level in both 1987 and 1997, but became insignificant in 1997. SOUTH, significant at the .05 level in 1993, also attained statistical significance in 1990 after dropping the influential cases.

Although removal of the influential cases affected the significance levels of several regressors, it is not clear that these observations should be eliminated from the analysis. Figure A1 in the Appendix shows plots of hat diagonals from each regression model after removal of the influential observations identified in Figure 4.3.

Figure 4.3: Hat Diagonals for Poisson Regressions

A. 1997

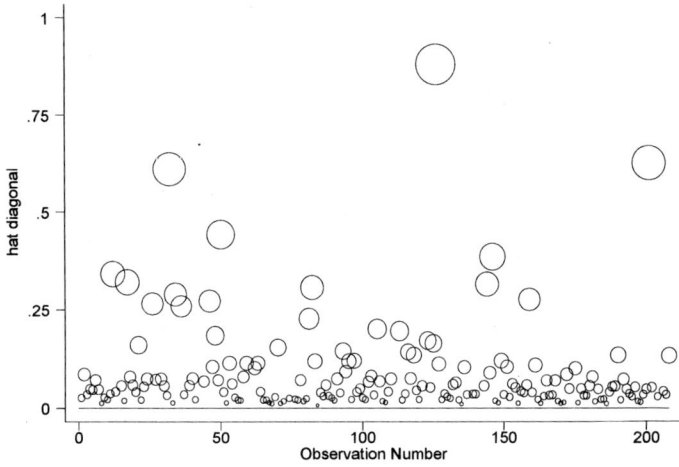

B. 1993

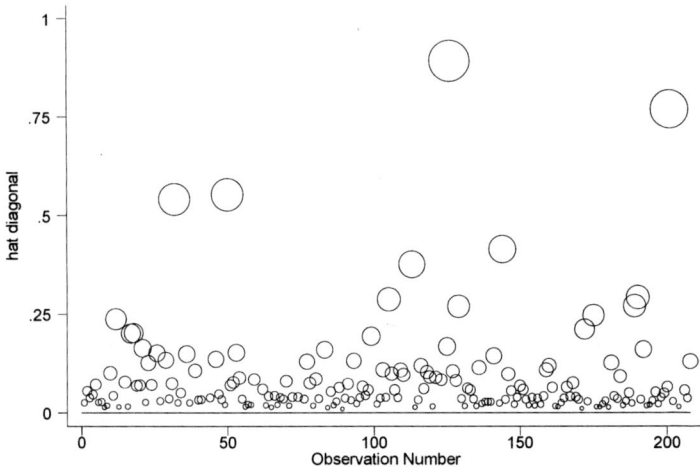

Figure 4.3 (continued) Hat Diagonals for Poisson Regressions

C. 1990

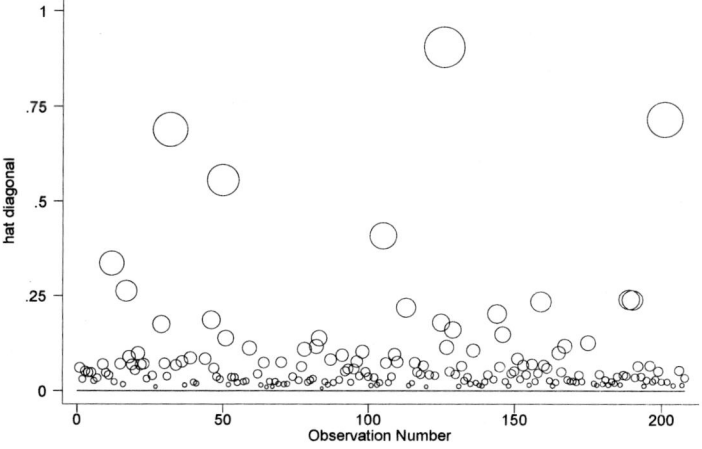

D. 1987

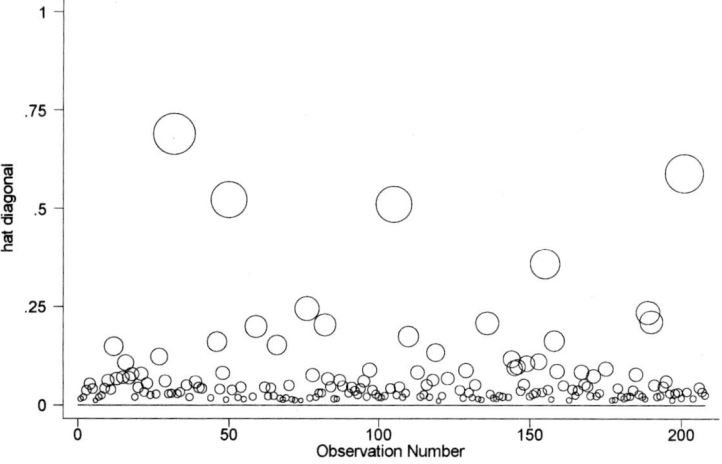

The pattern in 1997 suggests there are no observations that stand out from the rest, but the plots for 1993, 1990, and 1987 indicate new sets of influential observations, and it is likely that their removal would only result in the identification of new influential cases, and removal of influential observations could proceed iteratively until the sample size is adversely impacted.

Further, the influential cases are jurisdictions that have large values for population density, resource deprivation, field officer density, and arrests. Because of the interest in testing hypotheses regarding the effects of proximity and exposure to motivated offenders, these cases arguably should not be eliminated (see, e.g., Cameron and Trivedi, 1998:150-151).

Moreover, although $LR\chi^2$ statistics indicate that each model fits better than a constant-only model even after removal of the influential cases, doing so reduces the amount of explained variance by 43.8 percent in 1997, 13.6 percent in 1993, 32.0 percent in 1990, and 14.5 percent in 1987 (models not shown). Therefore, with a caveat that some of the estimates are sensitive to removal of certain observations, the decision is to retain all cases for analysis.

TRIMMED MODELS

Model 4 in Table 4.12 included a large number of regressors. To develop a more parsimonious model as well as reduce the number of missing observations, a trimmed model is estimated by eliminating those regressors that were not significant at the .05 level in at least one wave. Eliminated, therefore, are FOOT, UNIT1, SEMIAUTO, VEST, CHEM, ACADEMY, and COLLEGE. Regressors retained in the model are DEPRIVATION, DENSITY, STABILITY, FIELD2, ARRESTS, FEMALE, and SOUTH.

The trimmed model displayed in Table 4.16 shows DEPRIVATION is positive in all waves and statistically significant at the .10 level in 1997, and at the .05 level in 1993 and 1990. DENSITY is significant at the .10 level in 1997 and at the .05 level in 1987. However, the direction of its effect is opposite that predicted in three waves, i.e., is inversely related to homicides of police in 1997, 1990 and 1987.

Recall that population density was significant and positively related to homicides in all four waves in the proximity submodel that included the regressors DEPRIVATION, DENSITY AND STABILITY (Table 5.9). With the addition of the number of field officers per 10,000 population (FIELD2) it remained positive in all waves except 1987. When ARRESTS and FOOT were added to this model, DENSITY reversed direction in 1997 and 1990 (but not 1993), and continued to be inversely related to homicides in 1987. Further inspection of the models indicates the reversals of sign in 1997 and 1990 are due to the inclusion of ARRESTS, suggesting possible moderator effects between ARRESTS and DENSITY. This is explored below.

Regarding the remaining regressors in Table 4.16, the effect of STABILITY remains statistically significant at the .05 level only in 1997 and is positive in three waves, which is opposite the direction expected. FIELD2 continues to be positive in each wave and is significant at the conventional level in 1997 and 1987, and nearly so in 1990 ($p = .066$).

FEMALE is positive in all waves, but is significant at the .10 level in 1987 only ($p = .069$). Finally, SOUTH continues to be significant only in 1993, and shows reversals in direction across waves (it is positive in 1990 and 1993, but negative in 1987 and 1997).

The trimmed model continues to provide support for the hypothesis that proximity to motivated offenders, as measured by resource deprivation and the density of field officers, is associated with increases in opportunities for the victimization of police. There is also strong support for the hypothesis that exposure, as measured by arrests, increases opportunities for murders of police. The effects of the remaining regressors are less consistent, and DENSITY is more often inversely related to homicides. To explore this finding further, the trimmed model is reestimated with the addition of an interaction term between ARRESTS and DENSITY. The results are reported in Table 4.17.

With the addition of the interaction term, DEPRIVATION becomes nonsignificant at the .10 level in 1997, and changes from being significant at the .05 level to the .10 level in 1993. In addition, FIELD2 becomes nonsignificant at the .10 level in 1990.

However, the ARRESTS*DENSITY interaction term is less than 1.0 in all waves and it is significant at the .05 level in three out of four (the exception being 1997), indicating the effect of arrests depends on the level of population density in those waves. This suggests that arrests increase officer exposure to motivated offenders and risk of homicide, but that the effect diminishes at higher levels of population density. A possible explanation is that high levels of population density increase the probability of witnesses or intervention by third parties, which may prevent some attacks on police in the first place (deterrence), or by increasing the likelihood of prompt assistance may reduce the chance of serious injuries becoming fatal.

In general, the trimmed models in Table 4.17 fit reasonably well; the LRχ^2 statistics are all highly significant ($p < .0000$), indicating they fit better than a constants-only or naïve model. The pseudo-R^2 values indicate the amount of variance explained ranges from a low of 26 percent in 1993 to a high of 39 percent in 1987. Multicollinearity diagnostics using multiple linear regression indicates collinearity among regressors is not an issue (not shown). Further, an examination of residuals suggests no major problems (Figure A2 in the Appendix). There is one observation in 1987, however, that stands out somewhat from the others (deviance = 2.97). This is the Dallas Police Department, which experienced six officer homicides during 1986-1988; only the New York City Police Department experienced more officers murdered (N = 9) during that period. With zero officers murdered during 1995-1997 and 1989-1991, and two murdered during 1992-1994, the six officers killed in Dallas during 1986-1988 appear to be an anomaly that is not explained well by the model.

Despite the fact that the regression models fit reasonably well, the results are somewhat problematic in that several of the regressors are significant in some years at the conventional level but not others, and certain regressors continue to change sign across waves. Some of the inconsistencies in the obtained results may be ameliorated by pooling the data, which can substantially increase statistical efficiency of estimates (Sayrs, 1989).

GEE PANEL MODEL

Panel models, typically characterized as consisting of a relatively large number of units or subjects and relatively few time periods, offer a number of advantages over cross-section models (Cameron and Trivedi, 1998:275; Finkel, 1995; Sayrs, 1989:1). A central concern in estimating regression models using panel data, however, is that the assumption of independence of errors within observations is likely to be violated. If observations are correlated, estimated standard errors generally will be underestimated, leading to inflated Type I errors (Hsiao, 1986). Generalized Estimating Equations (GEE), however, is a useful method for the analysis of correlated panel data. GEEs are especially useful for repeated measures when the outcome is not normally distributed and the correlation structure of the repeated measures is unknown (Liang and Zeger, 1986; Zeger and Liang, 1986).

GEEs are used to model the marginal expectation as a function of explanatory variables (Horton and Lipsitz, 1999:160). In other words, in contrast to models that explicitly model subject-specific effects, GEEs are population-averaged models that measure differences in the response for a unit change in the predictor, averaged over the whole sample. These models are particularly suitable when the correlation is not of substantive interest and is merely a nuisance parameter (Lumley, 1996).

In addition to supplying the usual link and variance functions for estimation of general linear models, the within-group correlation structure or "working correlation" must be specified for estimation of GEEs, of which there are several alternatives. According to Lumley (1996:n.p.), little is known about the best way to choose the most appropriate correlation structure, but "it is possible to estimate regression parameters using any convenient or plausible assumptions about the true correlation between observations and get the right answer even when the assumptions are not correct. It is only necessary to use a 'model-robust' or 'agnostic' estimate of the standard errors."

There are two variance estimators available for GEEs; these are the *empirical variance* estimator and the *model-based* estimator. The empirical variance estimator—sometimes called the "sandwich" or robust estimator—is robust or insensitive to the misspecification of correlation structure and is asymptotically unbiased when the number of clusters is large (> 20), and the number of panels is small (5 or fewer) (Hardin and Hilbe, 2001:204; Horton and Lipsitz, 1999; Lumley, 1996).[39] The model-based or "naïve" estimator of variance is consistent when both the mean model *and* the covariance model are correctly specified. Since the correct covariance structure is usually unknown, the empirical variance estimate is preferred (Hardin and Hilbe, 2001:204; Horton and Lipsitz, 1999:162; Hosmer and Lemeshow, 2000:315-316).

GEE estimates may be robust to misspecification of the working correlation structure when using the robust variance estimator, but a moderate gain in efficiency is possible if one chooses a structure close to the true one (Lumley, 1996). Among the common choices, the *independence* correlation structure is the simplest, corresponding to estimating the regression coefficients as if the data were independent, and is not considered further. The *unstructured* option assumes the correlations between pairs of responses are different, and every element must be estimated from the data. The unstructured working correlation structure is useful when the number of panels is small, but is less suitable when the number of panels is large (Smith, Robertson, and Diggle, 1997:48). The *exchangeable* correlation structure assumes correlations between each pair of responses are constant for each observation, irrespective of the time separation. This is the default assumption of most statistical packages, and in practice gives good results in a wide variety of applications (Hosmer and Lemeshow, 2000:313). However, because observations closer together in time tend to be more similar than those farther apart, the first-order *autoregressive* (AR(1)) working correlation structure may be particularly appropriate for analysis of repeated measures (Lumley, 1996). Thus, an AR(1) structure is employed for the analysis.

Although it is assumed that the obtained estimates and standard errors are insensitive to misspecification of the working correlation structure, it nevertheless may be useful to check this assumption by specifying alternative correlation structures (Horton and Lipsitz, 1999:161-162). Therefore, estimates and standard errors obtained using the AR(1) structure will be compared to those obtained using the unstructured and exchangeable options.

GEE Results

Estimation of a GEE model using all four waves of data precludes the inclusion of the regressors unavailable in all time periods. These are FOOT, UNIT1, VEST, and CHEM (though VEST and CHEM are included in a three-wave panel model estimated later). In addition, upon estimating the initial model, STATA gave a warning message indicating that some groups had fewer than two observations, and that correlations for those groups could not be estimated. The problem appears to be associated with the pattern of missing data for SEMIAUTO (missing for 20 observations). No estimation problems were encountered once SEMIAUTO was removed from the model.[40]

Table 4.18 presents the results of the GEE regression model specifying an AR(1) working correlation structure. The interaction term between population density and the number of arrests, found to be significant in three of the four cross-section models, is also included in the GEE model. Since ACADEMY and COLLEGE do not contribute to the model ($p = .182$ and $.998$, respectively), they are dropped and the model reestimated. These results are reported in Table 4.19.

The trimmed model shows that DEPRIVATION, FIELD2, FEMALE and the ARRESTS*DENSITY interaction term are significant at the .05 level. SOUTH is marginally significant ($p = .054$), and STABILITY is significant only at the .10 level ($p = .076$). The Wald χ^2 test suggests a good fit to the data.[41]

The exponentiated coefficient for DEPRIVATION indicates that each unit increase in the resource deprivation component is associated with a 33 percent increase in the expected number of police homicides. Each 10-unit increase in the number of field officers per 10,000 population (FIELD2) is associated with a 19.4 percent increase in homicides.

Reestimating the trimmed model without the ARRESTS*DENSITY interaction term (not shown) indicates that each additional 10,000 arrests is associated with a 44 percent increase in murders of police. However, as indicated by the model including the interaction term, its effect depends on the level of population density, with the impact of ARRESTS on homicide risk declining at higher levels of density.

The percentage of female officers also appears to have a substantial impact on homicides. Specifically, the estimate suggests that each 10 percent increase in the percentage of sworn females is associated with a 39.4 percent increase in police homicides. The effect of SOUTH suggests unit location in a southern State is associated with a 53 percent increase in homicides.

Finally, though not significant at the conventional level, there is a positive association between STABILITY and homicides, and as in the cross-section models, the direction of the effect is opposite that expected. Recall, however, that this component consists of the percentage males aged 15-29 plus the percentage of the population still residing in the same household as in 1985, and they are inversely related to one another. Entering the original regressors making up this component one at a time into the trimmed model (not shown) indicates that residential stability is positively associated with homicides of police, but the effect is not significant at the .10 level ($IRR = 1.025$; $p = .143$). The percentage of young males is negatively associated, but it too is statistically insignificant at the .10 level (*IRR* = .931; *p* = .139). Why the effects are opposite that anticipated is unclear, but they are not consistent with theoretical expectations.

To determine which regressors have the strongest association with homicides, standardized regression estimates are examined (though the usual cautions about out-of-sample predictions pertain). Fully standardized regressors cannot be calculated, but semistandardized or "x-standardized" estimates can be obtained by standardizing the independent variables prior to entering them into the equation. Although not fully standardized, they are nevertheless useful for assessing the relative importance of regressors within an equation (Long 1997:15-17; Pampel, 2000:32-33). To obtain semistandardized estimates, the trimmed GEE model was reestimated after modifying the independent variables to have a mean of 0 and a standard deviation of 1.

Table 4.20 presents exponentiated semistandardized incidence rate ratios (*x-Std. IRR*), standard errors, and *p*-values for the model with and without the interaction term (Panel's B and A, respectively). For regressors significant at the .05 level, the results excluding the interaction term indicate that the variable ARRESTS exerts the largest influence on homicide (*IRR* = 1.44), followed in descending order of magnitude by DEPRIVATION (*IRR* = 1.42), FIELD2 (*IRR* = 1.25), and FEMALE (*IRR* =1.17).

When the ARRESTS*DENSITY interaction term is included (Panel B) and its estimate is adjusted to reflect an increase in the incidence rate,[42] DEPRIVATION has the largest effect (*IRR* = 1.33), followed closely by the interaction term (*IRR* = 1.29). These, in turn, are followed by SOUTH (*IRR* = 1.22), FEMALE (*IRR* = 1.16), and FIELD2 (*IRR* = 1.14).

It is interesting that the effect of SOUTH is suppressed when the interaction term is excluded from the model. To check whether the reverse is true, i.e., whether the effect of the interaction term depends on whether or not SOUTH is included, the model with the interaction term was reestimated without SOUTH (not shown). The results are virtually identical when unit location in the South is excluded, so the effect of the interaction term does not depend on whether SOUTH is included.

Because some regressors are just significant (FEMALE) or near significant (SOUTH, STABILITY) at the .05 level, sensitivity of the estimates and standard errors to misspecification of the working correlation structure is examined by comparing the coefficients and significance levels of regressors obtained using the AR(1) to those obtained using the exchangeable and unstructured correlation structures.

The results (not shown) indicate virtually no change in the estimate or significance level for STABILITY when using either the exchangeable or unstructured working correlation structures (IRR = 1.20; p = .074). For FEMALE, the estimated coefficient is virtually unchanged as well (IRR = 1.03), but the standard errors vary slightly with different specifications of the working correlation structure; the p-value increases in level of significance when the unstructured option is specified (p = .040) and decreases in significance when the exchangeable option is specified (p = .059). The significance level for SOUTH, however, increases when using the exchangeable working correlation structure (IRR = 1.57; p = .042), and it decreases when using the unstructured option (IRR = 1.52; p = .059). Thus, the p-values obtained for both FEMALE and SOUTH using the AR(1) structure are between those obtained specifying the other options. Although there is some slight sensitivity of the standard errors for FEMALE and SOUTH to specification of the working correlation, the changes do not appear to be so extreme as to alter the conclusions regarding their effects.

An additional concern regarding the estimated models is whether the conditional variance is equal to the conditional mean. Count data are frequently overdispersed, which violates the Poisson assumption of equidispersion (Cameron and Trivedi, 1998:77). Under these conditions, standard errors from the Poisson regression model will be biased downward and z-tests may overestimate the significance of regressors (Long, 1997:230). Although the individual cross-section Poisson regression models did not exhibit overdispersion, additional tests were performed to determine whether the GEE Poisson models exhibit overdispersion.

Table A4 in the Appendix compares estimates and standard errors from GEE Poisson and negative binomial regressions for the trimmed model presented earlier in Table 4.19. As can be seen, the estimates and standard errors are nearly identical. These results, plus a Poisson goodness-of-fit test from a maximum likelihood model of the pooled data indicate overdispersion is not a concern (χ^2 = 499.49; p = 1.0000).

MODIFICATION OF POLICY VARIABLES

Prior to estimation of the cross-section regression models, various steps were taken to check for errors in the data, and where reasonable, values were modified (see Table 4.4). I was reluctant to second-guess patterns in the police policy data provided by LEMAS when complete data were available, but several suspicious patterns became apparent when examining the values across waves. Sometimes policies or technologies were reportedly adopted in one wave, "unadopted" in the following wave, and then readopted in the next wave. Although such changes are not impossible, they seem improbable. It is reasonable to assume that policies and adoption of technologies are fairly "sticky" in the short term, i.e., that when new policies or technologies are adopted, departments are unlikely to reverse themselves within just a few years.

To test whether the failure of the policy-related regressors to attain statistical significance is due to possible errors in the data, the data were reexamined for improbable changes in policy regarding the wearing of body armor, educational requirements for new recruits, and the authorization/issuance of semiautomatic sidearms and chemical agents. The suspicious patterns and logical corrections are presented in Tables A5 – A8 in the Appendix, along with case identification numbers and city names (State abbreviations are included for city names that appear more than once in the dataset).

A simple logic was followed in modifying the values. When a policy first appears in a wave, it is assumed that the information is correct, and that once adopted by an agency, it is unlikely to revert in subsequent waves. Thus, for example, patterns of (0, 1, 0, 1) and (0, 1, 0, 0) would both be changed to (0, 1, 1, 1). Of course, there is no guarantee that the first appearance of a "1" is correct, nor that a policy did not revert. Nevertheless, this seemed the most appropriate recoding rule given these data.

The model shown in Table 4.19 is reestimated using the modified policy variables, and the results are presented in Table 4.21. As can be seen, modification of the policy regressors ACADEMY and COLLEGE does not alter the conclusions in that both regressors remain insignificant at the .10 level ($p = .180$ and .949, respectively). As in the model with the unmodified variables, SEMIAUTO had to be dropped prior to estimation when using an AR(1) correlation structure. Estimating the model using an exchangeable correlation structure with SEMIAUTO included (not shown) produces results similar to that obtained earlier; the effect of SEMIAUTO is in the expected direction, but it is not significant at the .10 level ($IRR = 0.789$; $p = .118$).

Limiting the analysis to three waves of data may mitigate the missing data problem associated with SEMIAUTO, and two additional regressors (VEST and CHEM) can be included as well. Therefore, a three-wave panel (1990–1997) is estimated next using both the modified and unmodified policy variables.

Estimation of Three-Wave Panel Model

Estimating the three-wave panel model continued to result in warning messages when specifying an AR(1) working correlation. The models are therefore estimated using an exchangeable correlation structure and robust standard errors. The results are presented in Table 4.22, with unmodified regressors appearing in Panel A and modified regressors appearing in Panel B.

Although the magnitudes of the policy-related regressors change somewhat when the modified variables are used, they all remain statistically insignificant at the .10 level (no $p < .242$). Therefore, the evidence continues to suggest that these variables, as measured, are not associated with officer risk of homicide.

SUMMARY OF MULTIPLE REGRESSION RESULTS

The results of the main effects cross-section Poisson regression models suggest most of the policing-related regressors are not associated with homicides of law enforcement officers. These are the percentage of officers assigned to foot patrol, the percentage of one-officer patrol units, the issuance or authorization of semiautomatic sidearms only, presence of a mandatory vest wear policy, the authorization of chemical agents for line officers, the total amount of academy and in-service training, educational requirements for new recruits, and the percentage of female officers. There is, however, strong support for the impact of arrests (positive and significant in all four waves), and some support for resource deprivation and field officer density (significant and positive in two waves). There is only weak evidence of effects of unit location in the South, population density, and residential stability/young males (each significant in only one wave).

With the introduction of an interaction term between arrests and population density, the cross-section results suggest that the effect of arrests depends on the level population density (significant in three of four waves), with the effect of arrests diminishing at higher levels of density. In addition, unit location in the South becomes statistically significant in a second wave with the inclusion of the interaction term.

Results using generalized estimating equations (GEE) are largely congruent with the results of the cross-section models regarding the effects of arrests and the interaction between arrests and population density. In the GEE models, both are substantively and statistically significant. Whereas the cross-section models provided limited or mixed support for the effects of resource deprivation, field officer density, the percentage of female police, and unit location in the South, the GEE model using an AR(1) working correlation structure suggests these factors are significantly and positively associated with homicides of police (though at $p = .054$, the effect of SOUTH is marginally significant). These results are largely insensitive to the specification of alternate correlation structures.

Table 4.1: Descriptive Statistics for Dependent Variable

Variable	Description	N	Min	Max	Sum	Mean	Std. Dev.
HOMICIDES 96	# incidents 1995-97	190	0	4	50	.26	.65
HOMICIDES 93	# incidents 1992-94	190	0	4	58	.31	.68
HOMICIDES 90	# incidents 1989-91	190	0	7	57	.30	.85
HOMICIDES 87	# incidents 1986-88	190	0	9	68	.36	1.03
Total # incidents '85-97		190	0	24	233	1.23	2.68
Total # killed '85-97		190	0	25	239	1.26	2.78

Table 4.2: Descriptive Statistics for Policing Regressors

Variable	N	Minimum	Maximum	Sum	Mean	Std. Deviation
UNIT1_97	190	9.50	100.00	------	85.9725	18.4112
UNIT1_93	190	1.32	100.00	------	85.6626	19.3517
FOOT_97	190	.00	63.64	------	5.1127	8.5615
FOOT_93	190	.00	56.24	------	5.6007	10.2770
SEMIAUTO_97	189	0	1	144	.76	.43
SEMIAUTO_93	187	0	1	108	.58	.50
SEMIAUTO_90	186	0	1	28	.15	.36
SEMIAUTO_87	178	0	1	10	5.62E-02	.23
VEST_97	189	0	1	80	.42	.50
VEST_93	189	0	1	57	.30	.46
VEST_90	188	0	1	35	.19	.39
FEMALE_97	190	2.60	29.32	------	11.0577	4.6589
FEMALE_93	190	1.53	25.74	------	9.6255	4.4460

Variable	N	Minimum	Maximum	Sum	Mean	Std. Deviation
FEMALE_90	190	2.25	22.81	-----	8.8320	4.1224
FEMALE_87	190	.99	19.13	-----	7.8551	3.6698
COLLEGE_97	188	0	1	53	.28	.45
COLLEGE_93	190	0	1	31	.16	.37
COLLEGE_90	190	0	1	24	.13	.33
COLLEGE_87	189	0	1	19	.10	.30
VEST_97	189	0	1	80	.42	.50
VEST_93	189	0	1	57	.30	.46
VEST_90	188	0	1	35	.19	.39
CHEM_97	188	0	1	173	.92	.27
CHEM_93	187	0	1	143	.76	.43
CHEM_90	184	0	1	138	.75	.43
FIELD_97	190	103	33513	167058	879.25	2680.87
FIELD_93	190	95	25130	145239	764.42	2122.29

continued

115

Table 4.2 (continued) Descriptive Statistics for Policing Regressors

Variable	N	Minimum	Maximum	Sum	Mean	Std. Deviation
FIELD_90	190	95	22496	140981	742.01	1970.19
FIELD_87	190	107	24757	137823	725.39	2082.28
ACADEMY_97	190	248	2424	231122	1216.43	397.63
ACADEMY_93	190	176	3096	224949	1183.94	411.20
ACADEMY_90	190	224	3120	225911	1189.01	482.79
ACADEMY_87	190	380	3440	212519	1118.52	469.29
ARRESTS_97	189	429	90130	946126	5005.96	8608.39
ARRESTS_93	189	558	96005	1040393	5504.73	9629.90
ARRESTS_90	189	617	112934	1143655	6051.08	11283.07
ARRESTS_87	189	467	112228	1000583	5294.09	10156.33

Table 4.3: Descriptive Statistics for Structural and Crime Regressors

Variable	N	Min	Max	Sum	Mean	Std. Deviation
POPULATION (size)	190	100217	7322564	----	331764.86	635954.73
DENSITY	190	133.3	23705.8	----	4312.424	3323.924
SOUTH	190	0	1	----	.34	.47
FHHKIDS	190	3.5	31.7	----	13.010	4.838
DIVORCED	190	6.48	18.64	----	13.0193	2.0998
INCOME	190	16925	56307	----	29089.77	7658.75
GINI	190	.326	.573	----	.44194	4.3924E-02
POVERTY	190	2.6	37.3	----	15.953	6.489
UNEMPLOYMENT	190	2.8	19.7	----	7.254	2.630
SEGREGATION	190	.135	.876	----	.51557	.17053
BLACK	190	.03	80.06	----	18.9575	17.63931
RSTABILITY	190	30.71	67.23	----	47.2581	7.1680
MALES15-29	190	9.04	22.08	----	12.9224	2.0257
CRIME_97	190	2513	355887	5889888	30999.41	41859.89
CRIME_93	190	3088	600347	6753789	35546.26	60548.07
CRIME_90	190	3334	710228	7009211	36890.59	67622.18
CRIME_87	190	3291	656509	6373901	33546.85	60450.54

Table 4.4: Poisson Bivariate Regression Results

	1997		1993		1990		1987	
	IRR (e$^\beta$)	R^2	IRR (e$^\beta$)	R^2	IRR (e$^\beta$)	R^2	IRR (e$^\beta$)	R^2
Policing Variables								
ARRESTS	1.00004[3]	.135	1.00004[3]	.137	1.00004[3]	.242	1.00004[3]	.257
FOOT	1.0336[3]	.030	1.0351[3]	.048	---	---	---	---
FIELD	1.0001[3]	.108	1.0001[3]	.109	1.0002[3]	.217	1.0002[3]	.218
UNIT1	0.9791[3]	.044	0.9847[2]	.027	---	---	---	---
VEST	1.7721[1]	.016	1.8351[1]	.018	2.0000[2]	.019	---	---
FEMALE	1.1283[3]	.085	1.1352[3]	.079	1.1629[3]	.094	1.1665[3]	.079
SEMIAUTO	0.6640	.007	0.7315	.005	1.5048	.005	0.2897	.008
CHEM	0.7803	.001	1.1795	.001	2.0417*.06	.014	---	---
COLLEGE	1.4328	.006	1.0685	.000	0.9683	.000	0.2711*.07	.015
ACADEMY	1.0001	.000	0.9993[1]	.016	1.0001	.001	0.9999	.001

	1997		1993		1990		1987	
	IRR (e^β)	R²	IRR (e^β)	R²	IRR (e^β)	R²	IRR (e^β)	R²
Ecological Variables								
POPULATION	6.18e-08[3]	.109	5.76e-08[3]	.113	4.80e-08[3]	.207	4.35e-08[3]	.225
DENSITY	1.0001[3]	.073	1.0001[3]	.090	1.0002[3]	.123	1.0002[3]	.143
DIVORCE	1.2882[3]	.052	1.1111*[.10]	.010	1.2391[1]	.037	1.1928[2]	.026
FHHKIDS	1.1091[3]	.069	1.0916[3]	.049	1.1129[3]	.073	1.0676[2]	.025
RSTABILITY	1.0899[3]	.080	1.0728[3]	.055	1.0959[3]	.089	1.0701[3]	.050
BLACK	1.0353[3]	.105	1.0345[3]	.105	1.0353[3]	.102	1.0224[3]	.039
SEGREGATION	267.8008[3]	.135	494.0296[3]	.169	869.9059[3]	.180	126.3184[3]	.108
MALES1529	0.7683[2]	.035	0.9855	.000	0.9203	.005	0.9444	.002
POVERTY	1.0783[3]	.051	1.0712[3]	.045	1.1029[3]	.087	1.0655[3]	.037
GINI (x 100)	1.47e+07[3]	.098	6.57e+04[3]	.093	3.10e+07[3]	.104	1.92e+07[3]	.103
INCOME	0.9999[1]	.025	0.9999[1]	.021	0.9999[1]	.020	0.9999	.008
UNEMPLOYMENT	1.1665[3]	.050	1.1570[3]	.050	1.2135[3]	.088	1.1572[3]	.044
SOUTH	1.2067	.002	1.5996*[.08]	.011	1.4318	.006	0.8797	.001
CRIME	1.00004[3]	.151	1.00001[3]	.137	1.00001[3]	.245	1.00004[3]	.274

Notes: 1 = p ≤ .05; 2 = p ≤ .01; 3 = p ≤ .001; * = p > .05 ≤ .10.

Table 4.5: Rotated Principal Components Matrix

Variable	Component		
	1	**2**	**3**
1) RESOURCE DEPRIVATION (Eigenvalue = 5.35; var. exp. = 48.6)			
Poverty	.91		
Fhhkids	.87		
Income	-.86		
Black	.77		
Gini	.76		
Unemployed	.73		
Segregation	.70		
Divorced	.65		
2) RESIDENTIAL STABILITY (Eigenvalue = 1.45; var. exp. = 13.2)			
Males1529		-.90	
Residential Stability		.78	
3) POPULATION STRUCTURE (Eigenvalue = 1.35; var. exp. = 12.3)			
Density			.86

Notes: Rotation = varimax ; total variance explained = 74.06%

Table 4.6: Poisson Bivariate Regression Results Using Principal Components

Component	1997 IRR (e^β)	R^2	1993 IRR (e^β)	R^2	1990 IRR (e^β)	R^2	1987 IRR (e^β)	R^2
DEPRIVATION	1.93189[3]	.085	1.83195[3]	.075	2.07944[3]	.103	1.65111[3]	.050
DENSITY	1.43875[3]	.035	1.60144[3]	.068	1.73246[3]	.092	1.69276[3]	.086
STABILITY	1.88888[3]	.062	1.34806[1]	.016	1.57932[2]	.034	1.57932[2]	.033

Notes: 1 = p ≤ .05; 2 = p ≤ .01; 3 = p ≤ .001; * = p > .05 ≤ .10

Table 4.7: Poisson Multiple Regression Results of Effects of Guardianship on Homicides of Police

Variable	1997 IRR (e^β)	1993 IRR (e^β)	1990 IRR (e^β)	1987 IRR (e^β)
UNIT1	0.9803[3]	0.9857[2]	----	----
VEST	1.6614*.087	1.7821[1]	2.1114[2]	----
SEMIAUTO	0.7141	0.7593	1.4805	0.2774
CHEM	0.7937	1.4910	2.1187*.052	----
ACADEMY	1.0002	0.9996	1.0002	1.0001
Constant	0.2725	0.1141	-2.3083[3]	-1.2208[3]
LL	-120.25	-132.65	-141.63	-144.45
LRχ^2	15.99; p = .007	16.08; p = .007	13.16; p = .011	2.58; p = .275
Poisgof	160.13; p = .88	175.53; p = .60	205.23; p = .09	203.45; p = .069
McFadden's R^2	.062	.057	.044	.009

Notes: 1 = p ≤ .05; 2 = p ≤ .01; 3 = p ≤ .001; * = p > .05 ≤ .10; constant is not exponentiated.

Table 4.8: Poisson Multiple Regression Results of Effects of Exposure on Homicides of Police

Variable	1997 IRR (e$^\beta$)	1993 IRR (e$^\beta$)	1990 IRR (e$^\beta$)	1987 IRR (e$^\beta$)
FOOT	0.98524	0.99411	----	----
ARRESTS	1.00005[3]	1.00004[3]	1.00004[3]	1.00004[3]
Constant	-1.64826[3]	-1.54081[3]	-1.68548[3]	-1.46240[3]
LL	-110.95	-120.85	-113.48	-129.50
LRχ^2	35.20; $p = .0000$	38.53; $p = .0000$	72.53; $p = .0000$	84.82; $p = .0000$
Poisgof	141.46; $p = 0.994$	153.94; $p = 0.959$	148.91; $p = 0.982$	169.48; $p = 0.816$
McFadden's R^2	.137	.138	.242	.247

Notes: 1 = $p \leq .05$; 2 = $p \leq .01$; 3 = $p \leq .001$; * = $p > .05 \leq .10$; constant is not exponentiated.

Table 4.9: Poisson Multiple Regression Results of Effects of Proximity on Homicides of Police

Variable	1997 IRR (e^β)	1993 IRR (e^β)	1990 IRR (e^β)	1987 IRR (e^β)
DEPRIVATION	1.72527[3]	1.72022[3]	1.90475[3]	1.56153[3]
DENSITY	1.35139[2]	1.56257[3]	1.67607[3]	1.64686[3]
STABILITY	1.73551[2]	1.20874	1.34710[1]	1.22947
Constant	-1.71597[3]	-1.49795[3]	-1.66979[3]	-1.32626[3]
LL	-108.30	-121.08	-119.69	-148.24
LRχ^2	40.94; $p = .0000$	41.07; $p = .0000$	60.70; $p = .0000$	48.05; $p = .0000$
Poisgof	136.24; $p = .998$	152.39; $p = .966$	161.34; $p = .904$	206.97; $p = .139$
McFadden's R^2	.150	.145	.202	.140

Notes: $1 = p \le .05$; $2 = p \le .01$; $3 = p \le .001$; $* = p > .05 \le .10$; constant is not exponentiated.

123

Table 4.10: Poisson Multiple Regression Results of Effects of Proximity + Crimes Known on Homicides of Police

Variable	1997 IRR (e^β)	1993 IRR (e^β)	1990 IRR (e^β)	1987 IRR (e^β)
DEPRIVATION	1.22298[3]	1.72555[3]	2.10096[3]	1.62096[3]
DENSITY	0.68367	1.12146	0.84641	0.76110*[.074]
STABILITY	1.68367[2]	1.06823	1.09634	0.96033
CRIME	1.00001[3]	1.00001[3]	1.00001[3]	1.00001[3]
Constant	-1.71597[3]	-1.68894[3]	-2.06289[3]	-1.76707[3]
LL	-98.59	-113.83	-101.53	-120.06
LRχ^2	60.36; $p=.0000$	55.57; $p=.0000$	97.02; $p=.0000$	104.42; $p=.0000$
Poisgof	116.82; $p=1.00$	137.89; $p=.996$	125.02; $p=1.00$	150.60; $p=.969$
McFadden's R^2	.234	.196	.323	.303

Notes: 1 = $p \leq .05$; 151.872 2 = $p \leq .01$; 3 = $p \leq .001$; * = $p > .05 \leq .10$; constant is not exponentiated.

Table 4.11: Poisson Regression Results of Effects of Proximity + Field Officers & Crimes Known on Homicides of Police

Variable	1997 IRR (e^{β})	1993 IRR (e^{β})	1990 IRR (e^{β})	1987 IRR (e^{β})
DEPRIVATION	1.35531*[.055]	1.52496[2]	1.76407[3]	1.10068
DENSITY	0.77884	1.08780	0.76287	0.58234[3]
STABILITY	1.57427[1]	1.02351	1.06090	0.81015
FIELD2	1.05952[2]	1.03240[1]	1.04164[2]	1.07851[3]
CRIME	1.00001[2]	1.000004[3]	1.00001[3]	1.00001[3]
Constant	-3.35799[3]	-2.29198[3]	-2.86425[3]	-3.22945[3]
LL	-95.29	-112.01	-98.31	-111.52
LRχ^2	66.96; $p = .0000$	59.20; $p = .0000$	103.47; $p = .0000$	121.50; $p = .0000$
Poisgof	110.22; $p = 1.00$	134.26; $p = .998$	118.57; $p = 1.00$	133.53; $p = .998$
McFadden's R^2	.260	.209	.345	.353

Notes: $1 = p \leq .05$; $2 = p \leq .01$; $3 = p \leq .001$; $* = p > .05 \leq .10$; constant is not exponentiated.

Table 4.12A: 1997 Poisson Multiple Regression of Combined Models

Variable	Model 1 IRR (e^β)	Model 2 IRR (e^β)	Model 3 IRR (e^β)	Model 4 IRR (e^β)
DEPRIVATION	1.34138[1]	1.42115[1]	1.30230	1.27166
DENSITY	1.03973	0.80181	0.72661	0.70232
STABILITY	1.57492[1]	1.53914[1]	1.54023[1]	1.54293[1]
FIELD2	1.07760[2]	1.06295[2]	1.06808[2]	1.06250[1]
ARRESTS	----	1.00004[2]	1.00003[2]	1.00003[1]
FOOT	----	0.97860	0.98690	0.99204
UNIT1	----	----	0.99527	0.99782
SEMIAUTO	----	----	0.71199	0.69485
VEST	----	----	1.21218	1.18006
CHEM	----	----	0.61374	0.66234
ACADEMY	----	----	1.00017	1.00022
FEMALE	----	----	----	1.03498
SOUTH	----	----	----	0.81975
COLLEGE	----	----	----	1.08251
Constant	-3.41843[3]	-3.25716[3]	-2.58222[2]	-3.15561[2]
LL	-99.94	-94.86	-93.60	-93.05
LRχ^2	57.65; p = .0000	67.28; p = .0000	68.75; p = .0000	69.84; p = .0000
Poisgof	119.53; p = 1.00	109.37; p = 1.00	106.84; p = 1.00	105.75; p = 1.00
McFadden's R^2	.224	.262	.269	.273

Notes: 1 = $p \leq .05$; 2 = $p \leq .01$; 3 = $p \leq .001$; * = $p > .05 \leq .10$; constant is not exponentiated.

Table 4.12B: 1993 Poisson Multiple Regression of Combined Models

Variable	Model 1 IRR (e^{β})	Model 2 IRR (e^{β})	Model 3 IRR (e^{β})	Model 4 IRR (e^{β})
DEPRIVATION	1.49635[2]	1.51701[2]	1.46259[1]	1.27663
DENSITY	1.43377[3]	1.21227	1.20890	1.54690[1]
STABILITY	1.11199	1.01175	0.99524	1.04132
FIELD2	1.04039[2]	1.03952[1]	1.04637[1]	1.02871
ARRESTS	---	1.00003[3]	1.00003[2]	1.00003[2]
FOOT	---	0.97914	0.97645	0.97103*[.069]
UNIT1	---	---	1.00120	0.99622
SEMIAUTO	---	---	1.00932	1.07356
VEST	---	---	0.96659	0.99193
CHEM	---	---	1.17121	1.28615
ACADEMY	---	---	0.99965	0.99936
FEMALE	---	---	---	1.04056
SOUTH	---	---	---	2.81552[2]
COLLEGE	---	---	---	1.69905
Constant	-2.28073[3]	-2.35382[3]	-2.25164[2]	-2.22400[1]
LL	-117.33	-109.61	-108.06	-102.66
LRχ^2	48.57; $p = .0000$	61.01; $p = .0000$	62.30; $p = .0000$	73.09; $p = .0000$
Poisgof	144.89; $p = .997$	131.46; $p = .998$	128.35; $p = .996$	117.56; $p = 1.00$
McFadden's R^2	.172	.218	.224	.263

Notes: 1 = $p \le .05$; 2 = $p \le .01$; 3 = $p \le .001$; * = $p > .05 \le .10$; constant is not exponentiated.

127

Table 4.12C: 1990 Poisson Multiple Regression of Combined Models

Variable	Model 1 IRR (e^β)	Model 2 IRR (e^β)	Model 3 IRR (e^β)	Model 4 IRR (e^β)
DEPRIVATION	1.66071[3]	1.75963[3]	1.60285[2]	1.48568[1]
DENSITY	1.51132[3]	0.78071	0.69974*[.065]	0.79479
STABILITY	1.26790	1.08026	0.97286	0.96951
FIELD2	1.03657[2]	1.03589[2]	1.03457[1]	1.02668
ARRESTS	---	1.00004[3]	1.00005[3]	1.00005[3]
FOOT	---	---	---	---
UNIT1	---	---	---	---
SEMIAUTO	---	---	0.46065	0.41110
VEST	---	---	1.48288	1.54046
CHEM	---	---	0.96252	0.99827
ACADEMY	---	---	0.99941*[.099]	0.99942
FEMALE	---	---	---	1.03308
SOUTH	---	---	---	1.65828
COLLEGE	---	---	---	1.27050
Constant	-2.35819[3]	-2.73759[3]	-2.06399[2]	-2.49241[3]
LL	-116.30	-97.97	-94.82	-92.99
LRχ^2	67.48; p = .0000	103.54; p = .0000	106.16; p = .0000	109.82; p = .0000
Poisgof	154.56; p = .950	117.90; p = 1.00	111.60; p = 1.00	107.94; p = 1.00
McFadden's R^2	.225	.346	.359	.371

Notes: 1 = $p \leq .05$; 2 = $p \leq .01$; 3 = $p \leq .001$; * = $p > .05 \leq .10$; constant is not exponentiated.

Table 4.12D: 1987 Poisson Multiple Regression of Combined Models

Variable	Model 1 IRR (e^β)	Model 2 IRR (e^β)	Model 3 IRR (e^β)	Model 4 IRR (e^β)
DEPRIVATION	1.14714	1.14317	1.15589	0.99630
DENSITY	1.35300[2]	0.57475[2]	0.66151[1]	0.66240[1]
STABILITY	1.05677	0.80792	0.88489	0.92227
FIELD2	1.06154[3]	1.07496[3]	1.05288[2]	1.04384[1]
ARRESTS	---	1.00005[3]	1.00007[3]	1.00007[3]
FOOT	---	---	---	---
UNIT1	---	---	---	---
SEMIAUTO	---	---	0.46925	0.55404
VEST	---	---	---	---
CHEM	---	---	---	---
ACADEMY	---	---	1.00050	1.00050
FEMALE	---	---	---	1.10603[1]
SOUTH	---	---	---	0.80236
COLLEGE	---	---	---	0.43252
Constant	-2.41016[3]	-3.12576[3]	-3.34157[3]	-3.89808[3]
LL	-140.83	-113.43	-104.63	-101.40
LRχ^2	62.87; $p = .0000$	116.95; $p = .0000$	81.57; $p = .0000$	88.02; $p = .0000$
Poisgof	192.15; $p = .344$	137.36; $p = .995$	123.80; $p = .996$	117.35; $p = .998$
McFadden's R^2	.183	.340	.281	.303

Notes: $1 = p \leq .05$; $2 = p \leq .01$; $3 = p \leq .001$; * $= p > .05 \leq .10$; constant is not exponentiated.

129

Table 4.13: Summary of Combined (Model 3) Results

Concept	Variable	Year			
		1997	1993	1990	1987
PROXMITY	DEPRIVATION		*+	*+	
	DENSITY			–	*–
	STABILITY	*+			
	FIELD2	*+	*+	*+	*+
EXPOSURE	ARRESTS	*+	*+	*+	*+
	FOOT			na	Na
GUARDIANSHIP	UNIT1			na	Na
	SEMIAUTO				
	VEST				Na
	CHEM				Na
	ACADEMY			–	

Notes: * = p ≤ .05; +/ – = p ≤ .10 ; na = not available

Table 4.14: Summary of Combined + Controls (Model 4)

Concept	Variable	Year			
		1997	1993	1990	1987
	DEPRIVATION			*+	
PROXIMITY	DENSITY		*+		*−
	STABILITY	*+			
	FIELD2	*+			*+
EXPOSURE	ARRESTS	*+	*+	*+	*+
	FOOT		−	na	na
	UNIT1			na	na
	SEMIAUTO				
GUARDIANSHIP	VEST				na
	CHEM				na
	ACADEMY				
	FEMALE				*+
CONTROLS	SOUTH		*+		
	COLLEGE				

Notes: * = p ≤ .05; +/− = p ≤ .10 ; na = not available

131

Table 4.15: Results After Removing Influential Cases

Concept	Variable	1997	1993	1990	1987
				Year	
PROXIMITY	DEPRIVATION			Δ^{ns}	
	DENSITY	*+	*+		$\Delta^{.10}$
	STABILITY	*+			
	FIELD2	Δ^{ns}			*+
EXPOSURE	ARRESTS	Δ^{ns}	*+	*+	*+
	FOOT		Δ^{ns}	na	na
	UNIT1			na	na
	SEMIAUTO				
GUARDIANSHIP	VEST				na
	CHEM				na
	ACADEMY				$\Delta^{.052}$
CONTROLS	FEMALE				$\Delta^{.104}$
	SOUTH		*+	$\Delta^{.026}$	
	COLLEGE				

Notes: * = $p \leq .05$; $+/- = p \leq .10$; Δ = change in significance level; na = not available

132

Table 4.16: Trimmed Poisson Regression Model

Variable	1997 IRR (e^β)	1993 IRR (e^β)	1990 IRR (e^β)	1987 IRR (e^β)
DEPRIVATION	1.33913*[.090]	1.43817[1]	1.62022[2]	1.03018
DENSITY	0.71144*[.093]	1.33087	0.86557	0.55504[2]
STABILITY	1.54993[1]	1.05888	1.06378	0.83458
FIELD2	1.05259[1]	1.00953	1.02772*[.066]	1.07051[3]
ARRESTS	1.00003[2]	1.00002[2]	1.00004[3]	1.00005[3]
FEMALE	1.04788	1.05398	1.04083	1.07758*[.069]
SOUTH	0.83444	2.06452[1]	1.56444	0.69324
Constant	-3.61430[3]	-2.68965[3]	-3.12820[3]	-3.09547[3]
LL	-94.36	-107.43	-96.54	-111.32
LRχ²	68.29; p = .0000	65.37; p = .0000	106.41; p = .0000	121.18; p = .0000
Poisgof	108.36; p = 1.00	127.10; p = .999	115.03; p = 1.00	133.13; p = .997
McFadden's R²	.266	.233	.355	.353

Notes: $1 = p \leq .05$; $2 = p \leq .01$; $3 = p \leq .001$; $* = p > .05 \leq .10$; constant is not exponentiated.

Table 4.17: Trimmed Poisson Regression Model Including ARRESTS * DENSITY Interaction

Variable	1997 IRR (e^β)	1993 IRR (e^β)	1990 IRR (e^β)	1987 IRR (e^β)
DEPRIVATION	1.32123	1.33052*[.093]	1.49282[1]	0.86892
DENSITY	0.75003	1.70888[2]	1.16442	0.79048
STABILITY	1.57937[1]	1.14982	1.18535	1.00096
FIELD2	1.05028[1]	0.99493	1.01377	1.04802[2]
ARRESTS	1.00004[1]	1.00005[3]	1.00005[3]	1.00009[3]
FEMALE	1.04281	1.05331	1.04479	1.10352[1]
SOUTH	0.88943	2.77380[2]	2.14638[1]	1.02860
ARRESTS*DENSITY	0.99999	0.99999[2]	0.99999[1]	0.99999[3]
Constant	-3.27718[3]	-2.73893[3]	-3.12501[3]	-3.69384[3]
LL	-94.26	-104.13	-94.48	-104.71
LRχ^2	68.49; $p < .000$	71.97; $p < .000$	110.53; $p < .000$	134.40; $p < .000$
Poisgof	108.2; $p = 1.00$	120.5; $p = 1.00$	110.9; $p = 1.00$	119.9; $p = 1.00$
McFadden's R^2	.267	.257	.369	.391

Notes: 1 = $p \leq .05$; 2 = $p \leq .01$; 3 = $p \leq .001$; * = $p > .05 \leq .10$; constant is not exponentiated.

Table 4.18: GEE Poisson Regression Results

Variable	IRR (e$^\beta$)	Std. Err.	P>|z|
DEPRIVATION	1.31892	0.12469	0.003
DENSITY	1.08078	0.14590	0.565
STABILITY	1.18722	0.11938	0.088
FIELD2	1.01802	0.00816	0.026
ARRESTS	1.00006	7.44e-06	0.000
ARRESTS*DENSITY	0.99999	1.93e-06	0.000
ACADEMY	0.99980	0.00015	0.182
FEMALE	1.03184	0.01810	0.074
SOUTH	1.57450	0.34607	0.039
COLLEGE	1.00045	0.17805	0.998
Constant	-2.54165	0.28208	0.000

Wald χ²: 592.97, $p \le .0000$

Notes: N obvs. = 753; link = log; family = Poisson; scale parameter (α) = 1; correlation = AR(1); Std. Err. = robust standard errors; constant is not exponentiated.

Table 4.19: Trimmed GEE Poisson Regression Results

Variable	IRR (e^β)	Std. Err.	P>|z|
DEPRIVATION	1.32946	0.12480	0.002
DENSITY	1.08731	0.14444	0.529
STABILITY	1.19451	0.11949	0.076
FIELD2	1.01794	0.00791	0.022
ARRESTS	1.00006	7.98e-06	0.000
ARRESTS*DENSITY	0.99999	1.99e-06	0.000
FEMALE	1.03375	0.01740	0.049
SOUTH	1.53383	0.34026	0.054
Constant	-2.77426	0.20991	0.000

Wald χ^2: 509.33, $p \leq .0000$

Notes: N obvs. = 756; link = log; family = Poisson; scale parameter (α) = 1; correlation = AR(1); Std. Err. = robust standard errors; constant is not exponentiated.

136

Table 4.20: GEE Semistandardized Poisson Regression Results with and without Interaction Term

Variable	A. Excluding Interaction Term			B. Including Interaction Term		
	x-Std. IRR	Std. Err.	P>|z|	x-Std. IRR	Std. Err.	P>|z|
DEPRIVATION	1.424	0.130	0.000	1.329	0.124	0.002
DENSITY	0.861	0.104	0.218	1.087	0.144	0.529
STABILITY	1.089	0.109	0.396	1.194	0.119	0.076
FIELD2	1.245	0.069	0.000	1.143	0.067	0.022
ARRESTS	1.438	0.077	0.000	1.782	0.142	0.000
FEMALE	1.173	0.090	0.037	1.157	0.086	0.049
SOUTH	1.084	0.100	0.381	1.224	0.128	0.054
ARRESTS*DENSITY	----	----	----	0.778	0.054	0.000
Constant	-1.667	0.105	0.000	-1.690	0.101	0.000
Wald χ^2	$466.21, p \leq .0000$			$509.33, p \leq .0000$		

Notes: N obvs. = 756; link = log; family = Poisson; scale parameter (α) = 1; correlation = AR(1); Std. Err. = robust standard errors; constant is not exponentiated.

Table 4.22: Three-wave GEE Poisson Regression Results Using Modified and Unmodified Policy Variables

Variable	A. Unmodified Policy Variables			B. Modified Policy Variables		
	IRR (e$^\beta$)	Std. Err.	P>|z|	IRR (e$^\beta$)	Std. Err.	P>|z|
DEPRIVATION	1.42242	0.15458	0.001	1.41498	0.15395	0.001
DENSITY	1.19161	0.158431	0.187	1.18675	0.15894	0.201
STABILITY	1.24472	0.126937	0.032	1.23961	0.12447	0.032
FIELD2	1.00857	0.010126	0.395	1.00876	0.00966	0.362
ARRESTS	1.00005	6.69e-06	0.000	1.00005	6.91e-06	0.000
ARRESTS*DENSITY	0.99999	1.95e-06	0.000	0.99999	1.97e-06	0.000
SEMIAUTO	0.92129	0.13641	0.580	0.87064	0.12635	0.340
VEST	1.11401	0.20229	0.552	1.09367	0.20551	0.634
CHEM	1.05983	0.23896	0.797	1.18525	0.43934	0.647
ACADEMY	0.99979	0.00017	0.232	0.99980	0.00017	0.242
FEMALE	1.03656	0.02179	0.088	1.03781	0.02213	0.082
SOUTH	1.86617	0.42148	0.006	1.85191	0.41449	0.006
COLLEGE	1.21276	0.22491	0.298	1.20437	0.21405	0.295
Constant	-2.60174	0.43067	0.000	-2.69378	0.50533	0.000
Wald χ^2	652.70, $p \leq .0000$			614.06, $p \leq .0000$		

Notes: N obvs. = 556; link = log; family = Poisson; scale parameter (α) = 1; correlation = exchangeable; Std. Err. = robust standard errors; constants are not exponentiated.

CHAPTER 5

Discussion and Conclusions

This research contributes to the fields of criminology and public policy by drawing on criminal opportunity theory to develop a model of police homicide victimization, and by using more appropriate statistical methods than those used in most prior cross-sectional research. Specifically, using regression methods appropriate for the analysis of rare-event counts, this study assesses whether differences in the organization and activity of police departments across 190 cities and four time periods influence opportunities for the victimization of officers, net of social, demographic and economic conditions of the jurisdictions in which they are located.

The results of the analysis suggest that indicators of social and physical *guardianship* are unrelated to homicides of police. Rather, police *exposure* (arrests) and *proximity* to motivated offenders (field officer density and criminogenic conditions), the percentage of female officers, and unit location in the South account for much of the variation in homicides across the 190 departments. A discussion of the results of the analysis and their implications for theory and policy follow.

REVIEW OF BIVARIATE POISSON REGRESSION RESULTS

The initial step in the analysis examined the relationship of each independent variable to police homicides in bivariate Poisson regressions. The results suggest that few indicators of guardianship influence opportunities for the victimization of police in the expected direction. Specifically, the authorization or issuance of only semiautomatic sidearms, the authorization of personal-issue chemical agents, and total hours of academy training (field + classroom) were statistically unrelated to homicides of police in most years. The percentage of police assigned to one-officer patrols (reduced social guardianship), and mandatory vest-wear policies (increased physical guardianship) were statistically significant, but the effects were opposite the hypothesized direction.

Two other policing-related variables—the percentage of female police officers and a requirement that new recruits have at least some college education—were included as controls. The percentage of female officers was significant and positive in each wave, whereas the educational requirement was unrelated to police homicides in each wave.

Two available measures of exposure were associated with the outcome. Arrests for Part I offenses and the percentage of officers assigned to foot patrol were statistically significant and in the expected direction in all years for which data were available. This suggests that arrests and assignment to foot patrol increase officer visibility and accessibility to motivated offenders, thereby increasing their risk of homicide victimization.

Most structural regressors, used as indicators of proximity to motivated offenders, were significantly associated with homicides of police in most years. Significantly related to the outcome were population size, population density, percent divorced, percent of female headed-households with children, residential stability, percent black, black segregation, percent below poverty, income inequality, income, and unemployment. With the exception of residential stability, these regressors were in the expected direction. Statistically unrelated to police homicides were the percentage of young males and agency location in the South (though young males was significant and opposite the expected direction in 1997).

Two additional measures, also indicators of proximity to motivated offenders, were significantly and consistently related to homicides of police in the hypothesized direction. These are the number of Part I offenses known to the police and the number of field officers.

In summary, the bivariate analysis provides little support for the hypothesized effects of the measures of guardianship, but substantial support for indicators of exposure and proximity to motivated offenders. In the next phase of the analysis, cross-section submodels based on the opportunity theory concepts of proximity, exposure, and guardianship were estimated.

REVIEW OF MULTIPLE POISSON REGRESSION RESULTS

The large number of structural regressors used as indicators of proximity to motivated offenders, many of which are conceptually similar, raised concerns about multiple comparisons and multicollinearity. Therefore, prior to estimating the multiple regression models, principal components analysis was utilized to reduce the number of structural regressors into sets of interpretable factors. Three factors or components were produced. One was *resource deprivation*, consisting of indicators of economic strain, family disruption, and large and segregated black populations. A second component was *residential stability*, consisting of the percentage of young males and the percentage of the population still residing in the same home as in 1985 (inversely related). The final component was *population structure*, consisting of population density (population size was used in the construction of another variable, but otherwise loaded with density).

When these three components were entered into a Poisson regression model, resource deprivation and population density both exhibited significant effects in the hypothesized direction in all four waves of data. Residential stability was significant in two waves, but the direction of the effects was opposite that hypothesized in all models.

The number of field officers, also conceptualized as an indicator of proximity to motivated offenders, was added next to the proximity submodel. To reduce collinearity with the number of arrests (added later), field officer density was recalculated as the number of field officers per 10,000 population. This regressor was significant and in the hypothesized direction in each wave. Resource deprivation and population density continued to be associated with homicides in the expected direction, except that density was no longer significant in 1997 and it reversed direction in 1987. This model explained relatively large amounts of the variation in the outcome, with pseudo-R^2 values ranging from .17 to .23 across the four waves.

Offenses known to the police, another measure of proximity, was consistently significant and in the expected direction, but was excluded from further consideration for two reasons. First, it presented severe multicollinearity problems in subsequent regression models (e.g., with arrests), and second, given the choice of excluding crimes known or arrests, the decision was to exclude the former because of the interest in studying the effects of the structure and organization of police forces on homicide risk, net of structural conditions.

Included in estimation of the exposure submodel were arrests and the percentage of patrol officers assigned to foot patrol. Arrests continued to display significant effects in the expected direction in all waves, but the effect of the foot patrol variable dropped out. With pseudo-R^2 values ranging .14 to .25, this model also explained substantial amounts of the variation in police homicides.

Unlike the other submodels, the guardianship submodel performed poorly in all waves, explaining only .9 percent to 6.2 percent of the variation in homicides. The percentage of police assigned to one-officer patrols was significant in the two waves for which data were available, but as in the bivariate models, was inversely related to homicides and thus opposite the hypothesized direction. Similarly, the effect of mandatory vest-wear policies continued to be opposite the expected direction, being significant in two of the three years this variable was available. The effects of the remaining three guardianship variables were statistically insignificant and the directions of their effects were mixed. These are the authorization/issuance of only semiautomatic sidearms, the authorization of personal-issue chemical agents, and the total hours of academy training (field + classroom) for new recruits.

COMBINING THE MODELS

To assess their relative contributions in explaining police homicides, variables from the exposure and guardianship submodels were added sequentially to the proximity submodel. The percentage of female police, recruit educational requirements, and agency location in the South were added next.

In the model with all regressors entered (Table 4.12), few displayed consistent effects in direction and significance across all four waves of data. The exception was arrests for Part I offenses, which retained it significance and expected direction in all models. Field officer density was positive in four waves, but significant at the conventional level in only two. Population density was significant and positive in one wave, but insignificant and inversely associated with homicides in three waves. Resource deprivation and residential stability were both significant (and positive) in one wave only, as was agency location in the South. These three regressors displayed some inconsistency in the direction of their effects as well, each reversing direction in at least one wave. The percentage of female officers was positive in each wave, but statistically insignificant. The remaining control variable, a requirement that new recruits have at least some college education, was insignificant in each wave. Notably, none of the guardianship regressors were significant at the conventional level in any wave, suggesting they have no influence on police risk of homicide net of exposure and proximity factors.

Collinearity among the regressors was assessed for the full model and was found not to be problematic, but several observations exhibited a strong influence on the regression results (Figure 4.3). Their removal, however, reduced model fit and produced new sets of influential observations. Consequently, all observations were retained in subsequent analyses. Additional diagnostics indicated residuals were well behaved.

Because of the disappointing results of the individual guardianship measures, a summed index of three physical guardianship variables was created (indicators of whether agencies had mandatory vest-wear policies, issued/authorized semiautomatic sidearms only, authorized personal-issue chemical agents). It was thought that a reduction in risk might be observed among those agencies with the "hardest targets", i.e., among those that implemented all three policies versus than those that implemented one or two. However, this strategy also failed to uncover statistically significant effects.

TRIMMED MODELS

Upon estimation of the trimmed models, it was apparent that the direction of the effect of population density depended upon whether arrests was in the model. Because this dependence was not due to collinearity between arrests and population density, an interaction term was entered into the regression. The interaction was highly significant in three of four waves, and displayed an inverse relationship with police homicides. In other words, arrests increase exposure to motivated offenders and officer risk of homicide, but the effect of arrests apparently diminishes in more densely populated jurisdictions.

In the trimmed model without the interaction term, resource deprivation was positive in all four waves and statistically significant at the conventional level in two, providing some evidence that police proximity to motivated offenders and homicide risk increase with greater levels of economic hardship, family disruption, and large black and racially segregated populations. However, in the model with the interaction term, resource deprivation was significant in only one wave and it reversed direction in 1987, providing more limited support for an effect.

Field officer density was consistently positive in the trimmed main effects model. It was significant in two waves and nearly so in a third (p = .066), suggesting that greater numbers of officers in the field increases proximity to motivated offenders and their risk of victimization. However, this variable is significant in only two waves in the model with the interaction term, providing mixed support. Agency location in the South was positively associated with police homicides in three waves, but statistically significant in two. The remaining regressor, residential stability, was significant in one wave only and positive in three, which is opposite the expected direction.

The trimmed main effects models and those including the arrests*density interaction fit the data reasonably well, with the models including the interaction term explaining 26 percent to 39 percent of the variation in police homicides. Collinearity and residual diagnostics indicate no major problems, though the results for some regressors were sensitive to the removal of certain influential observations.

To summarize, the cross-section models with all regressors entered provide no evidence that the measures of guardianship, educational requirements, and the percentage of the force assigned to foot patrol— policy-related factors perhaps most amenable to change—influence risk of homicide when measures of proximity and exposure to motivated offenders are included in the models. In addition, the percentage of female officers was significant in only one wave, providing weak evidence of an effect.

In contrast, the variable ARRESTS (exposure to motivated offenders) is a much more important predictor, as evidenced by the consistently significant and substantive effects across all waves in the trimmed main effects model. The significant arrests*density interaction term, however, suggests its impact depends on the level of population density. Being significant in at most one or two waves, support is more limited for the effects of resource deprivation, residential stability, field officer density, percent female police, and agency location in the South.

It was anticipated that the use of statistical methods appropriate for rare-event counts and addressing the problem of multicollinearity would produce more consistent results than those obtained in past cross-sectional research on homicides of police. To a limited extent, this is true. For instance, research by Chamlin (1989) and Fridell and Pate (1995) generated inconsistent results regarding the effect of Index crime arrests on homicides of police (see Table 2.1), whereas the cross-sectional results in this study show consistently positive and significant effects for this variable (Table 4.10).

Regarding the effects of the other regressors, however, the results from the cross-section analysis in this study are similar to those obtained in prior research in that there is much inconsistency regarding statistical significance or direction of effects. This is more so, though, for the trimmed models with the interaction term entered than for the trimmed main effects models. Nevertheless, more consistency in results is desirable. Toward this goal, greater statistical efficiency of the estimates was sought by pooling the data and employing generalized estimating equations (GEE) .

REVIEW OF GEE PANEL MODEL RESULTS

Using all four waves of data limited the number of policing-related regressors that could be included in the GEE model. Therefore, to allow the inclusion of additional (but not all) policing variables, a three-wave model was also estimated. Further checks of the temporal patterning of certain policing regressors suggested some suspicious values. To test whether their insignificant effects were a function of possible errors in the data, the original variables were modified to be more logically consistent across waves.

Estimation of the four-wave GEE model with all (unmodified) regressors indicated that variation in number of academy training hours (field + classroom) across agencies and a requirement that new recruits have at least some college experience were both unrelated to police homicides. Replacing these two policing regressors with their "corrected" versions also failed to produce significant effects ($p > .10$).

Additional policing regressors available in the three-wave GEE model were indicators of 1) whether agencies required all officers to wear bulletproof vests, 2) whether agencies issued or authorized semiautomatic sidearms only for officers, and 3) whether agencies authorized the use of personal-issue chemical agents. Both the corrected and unmodified versions of the variables were tested. None of the regressors, however, were significant at the .10 level, lending additional support to the earlier cross-section findings of no effect.

Estimation of a trimmed GEE model (Table 4.19) provides strong support for the hypothesized effects of resource deprivation and field officer density (measures of proximity) and arrests (exposure). As in the cross-section models, the effect of arrests continued to depend on the level of population density, as indicated by the highly significant interaction term between the two regressors. Unlike in the cross-section models, however, the GEE results indicate the percentage of female officers is significantly associated with homicides of police. The effect of agency location in the South was marginally significant (p = .054) and in the expected direction in the model including the interaction term, but was nonsignificant in the model without the interaction term. These results are largely insensitive to specification of the working correlation structure.

A review of semistandardized estimates in the model excluding the interaction term suggests arrests have the largest impact on police homicides, followed closely in magnitude by resource deprivation. These were followed in descending order of magnitude by field officer density and the percentage of sworn females. In the model with the interaction term, resource deprivation has the largest impact, followed closely by the arrest*density interaction term, agency location in the South, the percentage of female police, and field officer density.

To summarize, the results of the GEE models confirm the earlier findings that variation in the indicators of guardianship, percentage of officers assigned to foot patrol, and police educational requirements have no statistically significant effects on officer risk of homicide. Unlike in the individual cross-sectional models, however, there is strong support for the effects of exposure (arrests) and proximity to motivated offenders (resource deprivation, field officer density). The GEE results also indicate that the percentage of females employed and agency location in the South are positively associated with police homicide risk (though the latter effect was sensitive to whether the arrest*density interaction term was included).

IMPLICATIONS, LIMITATIONS AND FUTURE DIRECTIONS

There are four major findings in this study. First, most policing-related factors (measures of guardianship, education, foot patrol) are statistically unrelated to police homicide victimization. Second, arrests for serious crime (exposure) and the number of police assigned to field duties (a component of proximity) are policing-related factors that impact homicide risk. Third, criminogenic conditions (another component of proximity) or the ecological context in which policing takes place is an important determinant of risk. Fourth, two of the control variables—the percentage of female police employed and unit location in the South—are positively associated with homicides of officers. The implications of these findings are discussed below.

This study provides substantial support for the hypotheses, derived from criminal opportunity theory, that arrests for serious offenses, greater field officer density, and "concentrated disadvantage" (high levels of economic deprivation and inequality, family disruption, large and racially segregated black populations) increase police exposure and proximity to motivated offenders, which in turn increase police homicide risk. That these effects are statistically significant and substantive, whereas the indicators of social and physical guardianship and other police-performance factors (education) are noncontributory, lends support to arguments that violence against the police is largely a function of differences in community characteristics (Kieselhorst, 1974).

This suggests that meaningful reductions in homicides of police may be best achieved through decreases in levels of poverty, economic inequality, family disintegration, and racial segregation rather than through improvements in police performance. However, as clarified below, concerns over the reliability and validity of some of the policing guardianship and performance measures undermines confidence in tests of their effects. Obtaining and testing improved measures, therefore, is critical not only for informing policy and practice to enhance officer safety, but for further theoretical developments regarding the determinants of police homicides as well.

Although the findings in this study are congruent with Kieselhorst's (1974) arguments, that the number of police deployed in the field and arrests for serious crimes are associated with increased risk of homicide net of structural influences indicates that police homicide risk is also determined by organizational arrangements and not just conditions external to law enforcement agencies. In other words, controlling for structural conditions, this research suggests that enforcement initiatives to increase arrests for serious crimes and deploying more officers in the field increase officer exposure and proximity to motivated offenders, thereby increasing the probability of officer victimization.

The practical implications of these findings, however, are not so clear. There are undoubtedly many determinants of arrest productivity and police deployment patterns (e.g., resources, community demands, crime levels), and an administrator's awareness that increasing arrests and the number of officers in the field increases risk is not likely to be a major consideration. After all, assault, injury, and death are assumed occupational hazards of policing, and although substantial resources are expended to minimize their occurrence, intentional reductions in deployment or arrest productivity to increase officer safety is unlikely to be a viable strategy. Empirically and theoretically, however, this study indicates these factors are important, and researchers attempting to explain differences in police homicide risk across geographical areas should include measures of officer density and arrests in addition to community-level correlates.

Paradoxically, although this study indicates that increases in field officer density and serious crime are associated with increased risk of homicide, other research shows that increases in the number of police can, over time, reduce levels of serious crime (Marvell and Moody, 1996). Thus, future research using longitudinal designs might examine how police homicide risk varies with initial increases in the number of police "at risk," the impact of their greater numbers on levels of crime, and subsequent homicide risk.

That the measures of physical and social guardianship, the percentage of officers assigned to foot patrol, and educational requirements for recruits are unrelated to officer risk of homicide is disappointing. The finding of non-significant effects, however, may nevertheless be important for policy purposes because it suggests, for instance, that administrative decisions regarding deployment (e.g., ratio of one to two-officer patrols) may be based on factors unrelated to safety, such as efficiency, productivity, and cost.

Finding no statistical evidence of effects, however, does not mean that relationships do not exist. Several of the policing regressors employed in this study are only rough proxy measures of the concepts they are intended to represent, and limitations of several measures may account for their lack of statistical significance. An example is the measure of body armor usage. There is no doubt that body armor saves officers' lives (*Law enforcement officers killed and assaulted*, 1994:7; Knight and Brierley, 1998:23), but empirical studies attempting to demonstrate this in the aggregate have been unsuccessful (Lott, 2000; Kaminski and Marvell, 2002), raising concerns regarding the reliability and construct validity of the measures used. In this study, using the presence of mandatory vest-wear policies as an indicator of target hardening (physical guardianship) does not tell us how these policies are enforced or about actual vest wear rates.

Total training time may reflect poorly the proportion of time devoted to training for "officer survival" (e.g., shooting skills, defensive tactics, conflict management or mediation skills, approaches to potentially violent situations). Accurate measures of the relevant training would provide a better indicator of the concept being measured. Further, the measure of training employed in this study does not consider whether or how much *in-service* training is required for officers, which may substantially affect levels of skill acquisition and retention (Schendel, Shields, and Katz, 1978). Measures of college educational requirements and the amount of academy training may be relevant for recruits hired after 1986, but they may not apply to officers still on the force hired prior to that time.

Further, although attempts were made to "correct" for apparent inconsistent patterns in the LEMAS data and regression models reestimated using the corrected variables, there are no assurances that the modifications were an improvement. Until more reliable and valid measures are obtained and their impacts assessed, the results obtained regarding the proxy measures in this study must be interpreted with caution.

Another interesting though controversial finding in this study is the association between the percentage of female police and homicides. Historically, it was believed that hiring more women officers would increase the risk of injury or death to police because women are physically weaker than men and are less able to maintain authority when challenged (Grennan, 1987; Hale and Wyland, 1993). Even recently, Lott (2000:241) suggested that female officers are assaulted more frequently because they are physically weaker than male officers. Thus, despite contemporary arguments to the contrary (*Gender differences*, 2000; Lonsway, 2001; *Police use of excessive force*, 1999), the belief that hiring female officers may increase victimization risk continues to be held by some researchers.

The finding of a significant and substantive relationship between police homicides and the percentage of female officers adds support to the increased risk hypothesis. However, it is possible that this relationship is spurious, i.e., that it is due to a third variable related to both the percentage of females and homicides. One possibility is that police departments that strongly embrace the ideals of community policing hire more women *and* experience more officers killed feloniously in the line of duty. Springer (1994:9) argues, for example, that community policing "places a premium on specific qualities, such as being personable, even-tempered, and service-oriented. In addition, these officers must possess good communication and problem-solving skills and be conservative in the use of force... However, these qualities describe not only a good candidate for community policing but also an excellent candidate to be killed in the line of duty."

Thus, police administrators who strongly endorse the principals of community policing may attract and hire more women because they are believed to have characteristics more compatible with community policing ideals, e.g., female officers are less authoritarian and more likely to rely on verbal skills and mediation than physical force to resolve conflict than are male officers (*Gender differences*, 2000; Lonsway, 2001; *Police use of excessive force*, 1999). These qualities may be endorsed, promoted, and rewarded on a department-wide basis. If so, it may not be the proportion of women *per se* on the force that is related to officer victimization, but rather an organizational climate or culture that embraces and promotes community policing ideals. Further investigation of whether the proportion of women in policing, the degree of community policing, or some other as of yet unmeasured organizational characteristic of municipal police departments experiencing high homicide rates is warranted.

The relationship of police homicides to agency location in the South warrants further examination as well. Prior research suggesting a relationship, whether due to a violent southern culture, greater economic disadvantage, or other reasons, is not supported empirically (Bailey and Peterson, 1987; Fridell and Pate, 1995; Peterson and Bailey, 1988; but see Kaminski, Jefferis and Chanhatasilpa, 2000). This study produced similar findings in that location in the South was unrelated or inconsistently related to police homicides in the individual cross-sectional regression models. The evidence of no relationship was further bolstered by the nonsignificant results obtained in the trimmed, main-effects GEE model. However, when the interaction term between arrests and population density was added, there was evidence that unit location in the South is related to police homicide risk. Therefore, the effect of this variable may be particularly sensitive to model specification, and warrants careful attention in future research.

Although this research did not focus on the effects of crime because of concerns about multicollinearity, the individual cross-section regression results indicate Part I offenses known to the police are significantly related to homicide of officers, net of the effects of resource deprivation, population density, residential stability, and field officer density (Tables 4.10 and 4.11). This finding is important because it differs from results obtained in prior research (Bailey and Peterson, 1987; Chamlin, 1989; Peterson and Bailey, 1988). Two studies found no evidence of an effect, leading the authors in both studies to conclude that "police killings are not tied to the level of serious crime, and thus are not simply an expected cost of doing police work" (Peterson and Bailey, 1988:230; see also Bailey and Peterson, 1987:18). In the third study, it was hypothesized that higher levels of serious crime would increase opportunities for killings of police. However, although Chamlin (1989:358) found significant effects in three of six regression models estimated, the directions of the effects were opposite that expected in all models.

In contrast, this study found that high levels of serious crime increase opportunities for homicides of police, and contrary to the conclusion reached by Bailey and Peterson (1987) and Peterson and Bailey (1988), suggests fatalities incurred while fighting crime may be considered an "expected cost" of police work. Whether these contradictory results are due to the units of analysis used (States versus agencies/cities), method of analysis (linear versus Poisson regression), or because of other specification issues is unknown, but it would be useful to discover the reasons for the differences in future comparative analyses.

Future research might further build upon the present study by addressing a number of additional methodological and theoretical issues. Nonlinear relationships, for example, are not examined in this study, and except for the arrest*density interaction, interrelationships among regressors are unexplored. Including additional interaction terms and/or nonlinear effects may uncover important relationships not observed when examining only linear and main effects.

It is essential, of course, that theory guides such analyses. Unfortunately, theory regarding homicides of police is not well developed (Bailey, 1982; Chamlin, 1989). Although this study contributes to an understanding of the determinants of police homicides by drawing on opportunity theory and incorporating relevant variables from different theoretical perspectives into a single model (e.g., social disorganization and opportunity theory), there is no attempt at formal theoretical integration of measures of concepts.

Theoretical integration may be accomplished one way by positing interaction effects across the different theories (Miethe and Meier, 1994; Smith, Frazee, and Davison, 2000). This study included interaction effects between arrests and population density, but this was motivated by empirical results suggesting an interrelation, and not prior theory. Nevertheless, that the effect of arrests depends on the level of population density highlights the importance of developing formal propositions regarding the interrelationships of concepts from the different theories in future work.

Another methodological direction for future research concerns endogeneity or reciprocal effects, which have not been addressed in prior research on violence against the police. In this study, for instance, it is assumed that certain policies or practices influence officer risk of homicide, but what is unknown is whether the murder of a police officer or a cluster of murders impacts departmental practices, tactics, training, adoption of new technologies, and so forth, designed to enhance officer safety. Reciprocal effects may account for the positive and nonsignificant associations observed between some of the guardianship variables and police homicides in this study, such as mandatory vest-wear policies. Although difficult even with longitudinal data, prospective panel designs may make this feasible (Menard, 1991:23-24).

The use of police homicides as a dependent variable may be considered both a strength and a limitation of this study. It is a strength because police homicides are measured with very little error. However, its limitation is that it fails to capture many other forms of violence directed at police, such as shots fired at officers, woundings, aggravated assaults, and so forth. Although issues of data quality would need to be addressed (Margarita, 1980c), the inclusion of these incidents in the dependent variable would more completely reflect levels of violence against police (Cardarelli, 1968). Further, because the number of events would increase substantially, another potential benefit would be the ability to study levels of serious violence against the police at lower levels of geographical aggregation, such as police reporting areas, census tracts, or block groups, where substantial within-unit variation may be observed (e.g., Messner and Tardiff, 1986; Sherman, Gartin, and Berger, 1989).

To conclude, this study provides substantial support for the utility of opportunity theory as a theoretical framework for analyzing homicides of police. A considerable amount of cross-unit variation in the dependent variable was accounted for by indicators of proximity (criminogenic conditions and field officer density) and exposure (arrests) to motivated offenders, which are thought to impact opportunities for the victimization of police. The percentage of female police officers and unit location in the South also appear to be associated with opportunities for murders of police, though further research is needed to confirm their effects. Contrary to expectations, there is no evidence that the various measures of social and physical guardianship, educational requirements, and the proportion of the force assigned to foot patrol influence risk of officer homicide. But given the concerns about the reliability and validity of some of these indicators, future efforts to explain the geographical distribution of police homicides should obtain improved measures of these variables.

Endnotes

1. The terms police homicides and police homicide victimization are used interchangeably to refer to homicides of police, not killings by police.

2. Of course, not all things are equal, and although speculation, the effects of increased contacts and arrests on risk of assault and injury may be offset by a greater propensity for officers in "aggressive" agencies to use preemptive force that reduces their risk of assault and injury.

3. Calls-for-service data, available for the departments used in this study, were considered but rejected for use as an additional measure of exposure because the data appear to be highly unreliable (see also Klinger and Bridges, 1997).

4. An alternative hypothesis is that of no effect, as officers wearing vests may offset their protective effects by taking greater risks (Lott, 2000:258).

5. The subculture-of-violence thesis has been employed as well as an explanation for the high black crime rates in urban areas (Wolfgang and Ferracuti, 1967), which basically posits that some subcultures provide greater normative support for violence in upholding values such as honor, courage and manliness. Although measurement and design issues leave the debate unsettled, there appears to be more research support for theoretical perspectives emphasizing structural rather then cultural explanations (Parker, McCall, and Land, 1999:109).

6. Note that, although the number of officers assigned to field duty is conceived here as a component of proximity, at an organizational level an administrator's decision to deploy more officers to the field may also be considered a measure of "exposure", because reassigning desk officers to patrol, for example, presumably affects their "visibility and accessibility" to potential offenders.

155

Unfortunately, given data limitations, such conceptual overlap is unavoidable in the present study.

7.   Bailey (1982) found that the percent nonwhite population was positively and significantly associated with the police killing rate in 1964 and 1968 only; percent below the poverty line was positively and significantly related to killings in 1965 and 1971 only; percent unemployed was significant and positive in three years (1961, 1962, and 1966), and percent urban was statistically insignificant throughout the series (Table 3, p. 616). In examining the period 1973-1984, Bailey and Peterson (1987) do not include urbanicity and unemployment in their analysis, but percent African-American, percent below the poverty line, the state sex ratio, region (Bureau of the Census classification), and percent of the population aged 15-34 are included. The percent living below the poverty line is significant and in the expected direction for six of the 12 years; the sex ratio was significant in five years; region in two years; percent black population for one to two years; and percent population aged 15-34 for one year. The R^2 ranged from .16 in 1978 to .42 in 1979 (Table 4, p. 16). Bailey and Peterson next add one at a time to the above models the rate of violent crime (murder, assault, forcible rape, and robbery), property crime (burglary, grand larceny, and auto theft), and total index crimes; none of these variables were associated with killings of police in any year (Table 5, p. 19).

8.   Bailey and Peterson (1994) report that differencing removes problems associated with multicollinarity and corrects for the problem of unstable estimates often found in undifferenced models.

9.   In annual OLS regression analyses, Peterson and Bailey (1988) found that police homicides were positively and significantly associated with percent poverty and divorce rate in only two of the eight models (average amount of variation explained across the eight years was 32 percent). Percent black, racial income inequality, income inequality residual, percent urban, and location in the south were statistically unrelated. Collapsing the data into two four-year periods (1977 – 1980 and 1981 – 1984) to control for instability in the annual police killing rates, Peterson and Bailey again reestimate their models, but the results were unchanged. Finally, to these two models the authors added one at

a time the residuals of the general murder rate, violent crime rate, property crime rate, and index crime rate. These regressors were statistically insignificant, and the divorce rate and poverty continued to be the only significant variables.

10. To estimate the impact of the crack decade, a variable was constructed that is zero through 1984, a counter upwards for 1985-1991, level for 1991-1994, and then a counter downwards for 1994-98.

11. This variable is the percentage of the population in states with trauma systems; it is zero until 1976 and reaches 61 percent after 1995.

12. Body armor usage was approximated using two measures; the percentage of police killed feloniously who were wearing vests and a variable set to zero through 1972 (when body armor was approximately introduced) and a linear trend thereafter.

13. Of the six regression models, two contained all the variables, with one of these models estimated using OLS regression and the other using ridge regression. Variables were alternatively dropped and added in the four remaining OLS regressions in order to examine the effects of collinearity. Three variables were statistically significant in the full OLS regression model: the divorce rate, the percentage of families below the poverty level, and the Gini index; none of the variables were statistically significant in the ridge regression model. The total crime rate was significant in three of the remaining four models, as was the percentage of the population with Spanish surnames. The divorce rate was significant in two of the remaining four models, while the rate of FTE sworn officers, the percentage of the population below the poverty level, and the percent African-American population were significant in only one.

14. Indicators of the "general municipal environment" were a dummy variable indicating whether a city was located in the South, a poverty index (comprised of standardized scores of the percentage of families below the poverty level, the Gini index of income inequality, and the percentage of the population that was African-American or Hispanic), population density, and percentage of the population aged 15 to 34. As indicators of the "crime environment", Fridell and Pate included the rate of violent and property crimes per 100,000, a three-item index of gun-related

crime based on standardized scores of the percent of: (1) homicides committed with guns, (2) aggravated assaults committed with guns, and (3) the percent of robberies committed with guns. They also included indicators of the "agency environment". These were the number of violent and property crime arrests per 100,000 sworn officers as a measure of activity, the percent of officers injured during assaults as a measure of the dangerousness of the department, and the inverse of the number of sworn officer multiplied by 100,000 to adjust for "possible bias introduced by including both independent and dependent variables with the same denominator, in this case, the number of sworn officers" (p. 14). There were four statistically significant predictors in the 1977-1984: the violent crime rate, the gun crime index, the number of property crime arrests per 100,000 sworn officers (all positively associated), and the number of violent crime arrests per 100,000 officers (inversely related). Except for the violent crime rate, different variables were related to killings of police in the second model (1985-1992). These were the poverty index and population density (both inversely associated).

15. The three non-homicide models consisted of a demand equation as a function of real police wages, real public income, and crime rates; a supply equation as a function of real police wages, relative homicide risk, relative accident risk, risk of injurious assault, and factory worker earnings; and a relative accident risk equation as a function of police real wages and the number of vehicle miles driven in the population per capita.

16. Real wages of police is the average maximum salary for patrol officers, corrected for the Consumer Price Index (Southwick, 1998:601).

17. Age was coded less than 30, 30-54, and 55 and older; race was coded black, white and other.

18. The authors do not indicate whether the numbers of sworn officers used to control for unequal exposure are simply the number per agency in 1980 or some other measure, such as an average over the years from which the dependent variable was constructed (1981 – 1990).

19. The source and year(s) for the black mayor variable are not specified. Social, demographic, and economic data are from the 1980 Census. Crime data are presumably from the FBI's Uniform

Crime Reports (UCR) for the year 1980, but this is not clear. Killings of civilians by police are summed for the years 1980 – 1986 and are derived from FBI UCR data. Population size was entered with a quadratic term. Percent divorced was entered both as a continuous variable and categorically based on quintiles. Percent poverty, residential crowding, violent crimes, civilian homicides, robberies, and rate of blacks killed by police were logged.

20. An examination of condition indices in addition to variance inflation factors would have provided a more valid test of multicollinearity (see, e.g., Belsley, Kuh, and Welch, 1980).

21. Because reliable data on the number of police employed were not available for the period under study, Kaminski and Marvell (2002) used total population to calculate police homicide rates.

22. For the 190 municipal agencies used in this study (described later), the percentage of full-time sworn police assigned to field duties ranged from a low of 62.2 percent to a high of 99.1 percent.

23. Note that if an officer died from wounds in a year subsequent to the date of injury, the homicide was counted in the year the injury was inflicted.

24. The Bureau of Justice Statistics (Reaves and Goldberg, 2000:28) reports that municipal governments operated 86 percent of the more than 13,000 local police departments in 1997, but it is likely that the percent operated by municipal governments increases with the size of the jurisdiction served. Thus, the percentage of agencies serving populations 100,000 or greater that are municipal is likely to be greater than the 86 percent overall.

25. Generally, data is more often missing for cases in earlier waves. For the number of field officers, data were missing for three agencies in 1997, three in 1993, seven in 1990, and 21 in 1987. For percentage female sworn, data were missing for one agency in 1997, three in 1993, zero in 1990, and 20 in 1987. For total hours of academy training, data were missing for five agencies in 1997, five in 1993, seven in 1990 and twenty in 1987. For the percentage of one-officer patrol units, data were missing for seven agencies in 1997 and 14 in 1993. For the percentage of officers assigned to foot patrol, data were missing for 6 agencies in 1997

and 14 in 1993 (data for the last two variables are available only in 1997 and 1993).

26. Information on whether only semiautomatic sidearms were authorized/issued to officers was missing for two agencies in 1997, three in 1993, six in 1990, and 47 in 1987. Data on body armor were missing for three agencies in 1997, four in 1993, and eight in 1990 (no data for this variable are available from the 1987 LEMAS). For authorization of personal-issue chemical agents, data were missing for two agencies in 1997, three in 1993, and six in 1990. For the variable indicating that some college is required for new recruits, data were missing for two agencies in 1997, three in 1993, eight in 1990, and 18 in 1987.

27. There is one Census-based regressor in the analysis that was obtained from David Armstrong, Department of Sociology, The University at Albany, State University of New York. This is black residential segregation, calculated from 1990 Census data at the tract level for each city. In addition, there were six cities for which measures of black segregation were not available in Armstrong's data. These were Columbus, GA; Honolulu, HI; Indianapolis, IN; Jacksonville, FL; Nashville TN, and Providence, RI. Values for these observations were obtained from Karen Parker, Center for Studies in Criminology and Law, University of Florida.

28. The source for the Gini formula is Alker, Hawyard Jr. (1965) Mathematics and Politics, New York: Macmillan Company, as cited in Gini (1993).

29. In 1987, the LEMAS survey did not inquire about the authorization of types of sidearms; agencies were asked only whether they provided sidearms (or a cash allowance), and the type of sidearm (revolver or automatic). Thus, the data for this year likely under represents the number of agencies in which officers were carrying only semiautomatics. In addition, some agencies failed to respond to the survey question, with the greatest number of nonresponses occurring in 1987. Where possible, these values were filled in. For example, if in 1987 an agency didn't respond but indicated in 1990 that they issued or authorized revolvers, it seemed reasonable to assume that it also issued or authorized revolves in 1987. Thus a value of zero was substituted for these cases. In other cases, if reasonable deductions could not

be made the missing values were retained. There were only 3 cases for which data were missing in 1997 and 1993, 11 in 1990, and 55 in 1987 (based on the pattern of responses, 41 of the 55 missing values in 1987 could be reasonably deduced).

30. Some of the agencies' responses to this question over time appear suspicious. For example, some agencies indicated they had a mandatory vest-wear policy in 1990, but not in 1993 or 1997. A change from having a policy to not having one seems unlikely, but there is no way know that this didn't occur, and trying to logically deduce the correct pattern of responses seems risky in this case. Therefore, all responses remain as originally reported in LEMAS for the initial analysis. However, they are recoded for some subsequent regression analyses (explained in detail later).

31. Incidence rate ratios are interpreted in a manner similar to odds ratios, except that the response is a count (Hardin and Hilbe, 2001:132).

32. All count regression models are estimated using Stata, version 7 (StataCorp, 2001).

33. The Poisson estimates using the raw Gini metric produced extremely large values. For example, the incidence rate ratio (IRR) for 1997 was .000000460, and the exponentiated IRR was 14,747,291.55. Thus, the Gini was rescaled by multiplying by 100; this produced an exponentiated IRR of 1.1795.

34. Entering the two original regressors making up this component into the model (not shown) suggests young males (MALES15-29) drives the relationship rather than the variable residential stability (RSTABILITY). RSTABILITY in not statistically significant in any wave, while MALES15-29 is significant at the .05 level in 1997 and at the .10 level in 1987.

35. First-order correlations among CRIME and the principal components range from .207 to .306, and linear regression models produce variance inflation factors less than 1.20 and condition indices smaller than 2.25 in all waves.

36. For the 1987 model, the following interaction terms were tested one at a time; FIELD2*DENSITY, FIELD2*DEPRIVATION, CRIME*DENSITY, and CRIME*DEPRIVATION.

37. DENSITY is insignificant in Model 1 in 1997 but significant in Model 1 in the other waves; it is significant in Model 2 in 1987,

but not in Model 2 in 1990 and 1993. This does not appear to be due to multicollinearity, as an examination of collinearity diagnostics from linear models shows no variance inflation factor greater than 2.07 and no condition index greater than 10.04 (results not shown).

38. An additional strategy was pursued to test the impact of guardianship factors on homicides. This is the creation of a summed index of the physical guardianship variables SEMIAUTO; VEST, and CHEM. The rationale here is that line officers whose agencies issue or authorize only semiautomatic sidearms, have mandatory vest-wear policies in place, and authorize personal-issue chemical agents present more hardened targets to suspects and offenders than do officers employed by agencies that have none or only one or two of these policies in place. To test this hypothesis, dummy variables were created indicating whether agencies had no policy or one policy (low physical guardianship), two policies (medium physical guardianship), or all three policies (high physical guardianship). Because all three policies were present in only five agencies in 1990, the categorization in that wave is zero (low), one (medium), and two or three policies (high). Lack of data in 1987 precluded the creation of this index for that year. Compared to low guardianship, high guardianship (but not medium guardianship) is significantly associated with police homicides (IRR = 3.10, p = .022), but only in 1990, and only when other regressors are excluded from the models (results not shown). That the direction of the effect is positive may be a function of a greater likelihood of agencies implementing such policies in higher-risk environments. In any case, the physical guardianship index is unrelated to police homicides once other regressors are introduced, and provides no additional explanatory power over the individual items.

39. Actually, there are several versions of the sandwich estimator, e.g., the sandwich, modified sandwich, unbiased sandwich, and the modified unbiased sandwich. The modified versions are appropriate for correlated observations, and the unbiased versions have improved small sample properties (see Hardin and Hilbe, 2001:pp.27-31). Stata uses the modified version for GEEs by default.

40. Estimation of the model including SEMIAUTO and using an exchangeable correlation structure and robust standard errors (not shown) shows that the effect of SEMIAUTO is in the expected direction, suggesting that the issuance of semiautomatic sidearms may provide a protective effect (IRR = 0.819), but it is not statistically significant at the .10 level (p = .187).

41. Model diagnostics (e.g., residuals, influence statistics) available for cross-sectional estimators have not yet been extended to their GEE panel data counterparts in commercial software (Hardin and Hilbe, 2003; McDowell, 2001).

42. This is done by reversing the sign of the coefficient prior to exponentiation, and is necessary because exponentiated incidence rate ratios are not symmetrical about zero. The unexponentiated coefficient for the interaction term is -.251; reversing its sign and exponentiating produces an IRR of 1.285.

References

Adler, Freda, Mueller, O. W Gerhard, and William S. Laufer. 1994. *Criminal Justice*. New York, NY: McGraw-Hill, Inc.

Alker, Hawyard Jr. 1965. *Mathematics and Politics*. New York, NY: Macmillan Company.

Armstrong, David A. and O. Elmer Polk. 1999. Historical analysis of the role of higher education in law enforcement and its impact on police performance and career paths. *Journal of Community Policing* 1:67-85.

Bailey, William C. 1982. Capital punishment and lethal assaults against police. *Criminology* 19:608-25.

--------. 1984. Poverty, inequality, and homicide rates: Some not so unexpected findings. *Criminology* 22:531-550.

--------. 1996. Less-than-lethal weapons and police-citizen killings in U.S. urban areas. *Crime and Delinquency* 42:535-552.

Bailey, William C. and Ruth D. Peterson. 1987. Police killings and capital punishment: The post-Furman period. *Criminology* 25:1-25.

--------. 1994. Murder, capital punishment, and deterrence: A review of the evidence and an examination of police killings. *Journal of Social Issues* 50:53-73.

Balkwell, James W. 1990. Ethnic inequality and the rate of homicide. *Social Forces* 69(1):53-70.

Baller, Robert D., Luc Anselin, Steven F. Messner, Glenn Deane, and Darnell F. Hawkins. 2001. Structural covariates of U.S. county homicide rates: Incorporating spatial effects. *Criminology* 39:561-590.

Bayley, David H. and James Garofalo. 1989. The management of violence by police patrol officers. *Criminology* 27:1-26.

Blau, Judith R. and Peter M. Blau. 1982. The costs of inequality: Metropolitan structure and violent crime. *American Sociological Review* 47:114-129.

Blau, Peter M. and Reid M. Golden. 1986 Metropolitan structure and criminal violence. *The Sociological Quarterly* 27:15-26.

Block, Richard, Marcus Felson, and Carolyn R. Block. 1984. Crime victimization for incumbents of 246 occupations. *Social* Science Research 69:442-451.

Boylen, Max and Robert Little. 1990. How criminal justice theory can aid our understanding of assaults on police officers. The Police Journal 63: 208-215.

Boydstun, John E., Sherry, Michael E., and Nicholas A. Moelter. 1977. Patrol staffing in San Diego: One- or two-officer units. Washington, DC: Police Foundation.

Brantingham, Paul and Patricia Brantingham. 1984. Patterns in Crime. New York, NY: Macmillan Publishing Company.

Brearley, H. C. 1934. Homicide in the United States. Chapel Hill, NC: University of North Carolina Press.

Belsley, David A., Kuh, Edwin and Roy E. Welsch. 1980. Regression Diagnostics. New York, NY: John Wiley and Sons.

Brierley, William. 1998. 1998 Casualty reduction analysis. Paper presented to the FBI-National Academy Associates, Virginia Chapter, Roanoke, VA.

Bristow, Allen P. 1972. Police officer shootings – A tactical evaluation. In Samuel G. Chapman (ed.), *Police Patrol Readings*, 2nd ed. Springfield, IL: Charles C. Thomas.

Brown, Jodi M. and Patrick A. Langan. 2001. *Policing and homicide, 1976-98: Justifiable homicide by police, police officers murdered by felons*. Washington, DC: Bureau of Justice Statistics.

Burgess, Ernest W. 1916. Juvenile delinquency in a small city. *Journal of the American Institute of Criminal Law and Criminology* 6:724-728.

Bursik, Robert J. and Harold G. Grasmick. 1993. Economic deprivation and neighborhood crime rates, 1960-1980. *Law and Society Review* 27:263-283.

Cameron, A. Colin and Pravin K. Trivedi. 1998. *Regression Analysis of Count Data.* Cambridge, MA: Cambridge University Press.

Cardarelli, Albert P. 1968. An analysis of police killed by criminal action: 1961-1963. Journal of Criminal Law, Criminology, and Police Science 59:447-453.

Cascio, Wayne F. 1977. Formal education and police officer performance. Journal of *Police Sciences and Administration* 5:89-96.

Chilton, Roland, and Dee Weber. 2000. Uniform Crime Reporting Program [United States]: Arrests by age, sex, and race for police agencies in metropolitan statistical areas, 1960-1997 [computer file], second ICPSR version. Amherst, MA: University of Massachusetts [producer], 2000. Ann Arbor, MI: Inter-university Consortium for Political and Social Research [distributor].

Chamlin, Mitchell B. 1989. Conflict theory and police killings. *Deviant Behavior* 10: 353-368.

Chamlin, Mitchell B. and John K. Cochran. 1994. Opportunity, motivation, and assaults on police: A bivariate ARIMA analysis. *American Journal of Criminal Justice* 19:1-19.

Chapman, Samuel G. 1972. *Police Patrol Readings*, 2nd edition. Charles C. Thomas.

-------. 1998. *Murdered on Duty: The Killing of Police Officers In America*, 2nd edition. Springfield, Ill: Charles C. Thomas.

Chiricos, Theodore G. 1987 Rates of crime and unemployment: an analysis of aggregate research evidence. *Social Problems* 34:187-212.

Cloward, Richard A. and Lloyd E. Ohlin. 1960. *Delinquency and Opportunity: A Theory of Delinquent Gangs.* New York, NY: The Free Press.

Cohen, Lawrence E. and Marcus Felson. 1979. Social change and crime rate trends: A routine activity approach. *American Sociological Review* 44:588-608.

Cohen, Lawrence E., James R. Kluegel, and Kenneth C. Land. 1981. Social inequality and predatory criminal victimization: An exposition and test of a formal theory. American Sociological Review 46:505-524.

Collins, James J., Cox, Grenda G., and Patrick Langan. 1987. Job activities and personal crime victimization: Implications for theory. Social Science Research 16:345-360.

Cook, Philip J. 1986. The demand and supply of criminal opportunities. In Tonry, Michael and Norval Morris (eds.), Crime and Justice: An Annual Review of Research, Vol. 7. Chicago, IL: The University of Chicago Press.

Cornish, Derek B., and Ronald V. Clarke (eds.) 1986. The Reasoning Criminal: Rational Choice Perspective on Offending. New York, NY: Springer-Verlag.

Corzine, Jay, Lin Huff-Corzine, and Hugh P. Whitt. 1999. Cultural and subcultural theories of homicide. In Smith, M. Dwayne and Margaret A. Zahn (eds.), *Homicide: A Sourcebook of Social Research*. Thousands Oaks, CA: Sage Publications.

Crank, John P. 1990. The influence of environmental and organizational factors on police style in urban and rural environments. *Journal of Research and Crime and Delinquency* 27:166-189.

Creamer, Shane J. and Gerald D. Robin. 1970. Assaults on police. In Samuel G. Chapman (ed.), *Police Patrol Readings*, 2nd ed. Springfield, IL: Charles C. Thomas.

Ellis, Desmond, Alfred Choi, and Chris Blaus. 1993. Injuries to police officers attending domestic disturbances: An empirical study. Canadian Journal of Criminology 35:149-168.

Estey, Joseph G. 1997. Survivors' Club hits 2000." The Police Chief 64:19-20.

Felson, Marcus. 1998. Crime and Everyday Life, 2nd ed. Thousand Oaks, CA: Pine Forge Press.

Felson, Richard B. and Steven F. Messner. 1996. To kill or not to kill? Lethal outcomes in injurious attacks. Criminology 34:519-545.

Finkel, Steven E. 1995. Causal Analysis with Panel Data. Sage University Paper series on Quantitative Applications in the Social Sciences, 07-105. Thousand Oaks, CA: Sage Publications.

Fridell, Lorie A. and Anthony M. Pate. 1995. *Death on patrol: Felonious killings of police officers*. Final report. Washington, DC: National Institute of Justice.

-------. 1997. Death on patrol: Killings of American law enforcement officers. In Dunham, Roger G. and Geoffrey P. Alpert (eds.). *Critical Issues in Policing: Contemporary Readings*, 3rd ed. Prospect Heights, IL: Waveland Press, Inc.

Fyfe, James J. 1979. *Administrative interventions on police shooting discretion: An empirical examination*. Journal of Criminal Justice 7:309-323.

Garofalo, James. 1987. Reassessing the lifestyle model of criminal victimization. In Gottfredson, Michael and Travis Hirschi (eds.), *Positive Criminology*, Newbury Park, CA: Sage Publications.

Garner, Joel and Elizabeth Clemmer. 1986. *Danger to police in domestic disturbances – A new look*. Research in Brief. Washington, DC: National Institute of Justice.

Garner, Joel, John Buchanan, Tom Schade, and John Hepburn. 1996. *Understanding the use of force by and against the police*. Research in Brief. Washington, DC: National Institute of Justice.

Gastil, Raymond D. 1971. Homicide and a regional culture of violence. American *Sociological Review* 36:412-427.

Gauvin, Robert. 1994. *Oleoresin Capsicum Spray: A Progress Report*. Portland, OR: Portland Police Department.

Geller, William A. and Kevin J. Karales. 1982. Shootings of and by Chicago police: Uncommon crises part II: Shootings of police, shooting correlates and control strategies. *The Journal of Criminal Law and Criminology* 73: 331-378.

Geller, William A. and Michael S. Scott. 1992. *Deadly Force: What We Know*. Washington, DC: Police Executive Research Forum.

Gender differences in the cost of police brutality and misconduct. 2000. Los Angeles, CA: National Center for Woman in Policing.

Gini says: Measuring income inequality. 1993. Left Business Observer. Available at http://www.panix.com/~dhenwood/ Gini_supplement.html.

Greenfeld, Larry. A., Patrick A. Langan, and Stephen K. Smith. 1997. *Police use of force: Collection of national data.* Washington, DC: Bureau of Justice Statistics.

Grennan, Sean A. 1987. Findings on the role of officer gender in violent encounters with citizens. *Journal of Police Science and Administration* 15:78-85.

Hackney, Sheldon. 1969. Southern violence. American Historical Review 39:906-925.

Handberg, Roger, Charles M. Unkovic, and James Feuerstein. 1986. Organizational and ecological explanations for violence against the police: A preliminary analysis. *International Review of History and Political Science* 23: 1-14.

Hale, Donna C. and Stacey M. Wyland. 1993. Dragons and dinosaurs: The plight of patrol women. *Police Forum* 3:1-6.

Hardin, James and Joseph Hilbe. 2001. *Generalized Linear Models and Extensions.* College Stations, TX: Stata Press.

Hardin, James W. and Joseph M. Hilbe. 2003. *Generalized Estimating Equations.* Boca Raton, FL: Chapman & Hall/CRC Press.

Heskett, Sandra L. 1996. *Workplace Violence: Before, During and After.* Boston, MA: Butterworth-Heinemann.

Hindelang, Michael J., Gottfredson, Michael R. and James Garofalo. 1978. *Victims of Personal Crime: An Empirical Foundation for a Theory of Personal Victimization.* Cambridge, Ma: Ballinger Publishing Company.

Hirschi, Travis, and Michael Gottfredson. 1983. Age and the explanation of crime. *American Journal of Sociology* 89:522-584.

Horton, Nicholas J. and Stuart R. Lipsitz. 1999. Review of software to fit generalized estimating equation regression models. The American Statistician 53:160-169.

Hosmer, David W. and Stanley Lemeshow. 2000. Applied Logistic Regression. New York, NY: John Wiley & Sons.

Hough, Mike. 1987. Offenders' choice of target: Findings from victim surveys. Journal of Quantitative Criminology 3:355-369.

Jacobs, David and Jason T. Carmichael (2002). Subordination and violence against state control agents: Testing political explanations for lethal assaults against the police. Social Forces 80:1223-1251.

Jenkins, Lynn. 1996. Violence in the workplace: Risk factors and prevention strategies. DHHS (NIOSH) publication number 96-100. Washington, DC: U.S. Government Printing Office.

Kaminski, Robert J. 1997. Analyzing the structural determinants of killings of police: Does method matter? Paper presented at the American Society of Criminology, San Diego, CA, November 18-22.

-------. 1998. Toward an organizational—exposure model of police officer victimization. Paper presented at the American Society of Criminology, Washington, DC, November 11-14.

Kaminski, Robert J. and David W. M. Sorensen. 1995. A multivariate analysis of individual, situational, and environmental factors associated with police assault injuries. *American Journal of Police* 14:3-48.

Kaminski, Robert J., Eric S. Jefferis, and Chanchalat Chanhatasilpa. 2000. A spatial analysis of American police killed in the line of duty. In Turnbull, L., Hendrix, H. E., and B. D. Dent (eds.), *Atlas of Crime: Mapping the Criminal Landscape.* Phoenix, AZ: Oryx Press.

Kaminski, Robert J. and Jeffrey Martin. 2000. An analysis of police officer satisfaction with defense and control tactics. *Policing: An International Journal of Police Strategies and Management* 23:132-153.

Kaminski, Robert J., Steven M. Edwards, and James W. Johnson. 1998. The deterrent effects of oleoresin capsicum on assaults against police: Testing the Velcro-effect hypothesis. *Police Quarterly* 1:1-20.

-------. 1999. Assessing the incapacitative effects of pepper spray during resistive encounters with the police. *Policing: An*

International Journal of Police Strategies and Management 22:7-29.

Kaminski, Robert J. and Thomas B. Marvell. 2002. A comparison of changes in police and general homicides, 1930 – 1998. Criminology 40:701-720.

Kennedy, Peter. 1992. A Guide to Econometrics. Cambridge, MA: The MIT Press.

Kieselhorst, Daniel C. 1974. A theoretical perspective of violence against police. Criminal Justice Policy and Administration Research Series. Norman, OK: Bureau of Government Research, University of Oklahoma.

King, William R. and Beth A. Sanders. 1997. Nice guys finish last: A critical review of killed in the line of duty. *Policing: An International Journal of Police Strategies and Management* 20:392-407.

Klinger, David A. and George S. Bridges. 1997. Measurement error in calls-for-service as an indicator of crime. *Criminology* 35: 705-726.

Knight, Anna and William Brierley. 1998. 1998 Survivors' Club update. *The Police Chief* 65:23-24,26.

Konstantin, David N. 1984. Homicides of American law enforcement officers. *Justice Quarterly* 1:29-45.

Koper, Christopher S., and Darin C. Reedy. 2001. The impact of firearm types on gun assault outcomes: A comparison of gun assaults involving semiautomatic handguns and revolvers. Unpublished manuscript.

Kornhauser, Ruth. 1978. *Social Sources of Delinquency*. Chicago: University of Chicago Press.

Kovandzic, Tomislav V., Lynne M. Vieraitis, and Mark R. Yeisley. 1998. The structural covariates of urban homicide: Reassessing the impact of income inequality and poverty in the post-Reagan era. *Criminology* 36:569-599.

Krivo, Lauren J. and Ruth D. Peterson. 1996. Extremely disadvantaged neighborhood and urban crime. *Social Forces* 75:619-650.

Land, Kenneth C., Patricia L. McCall, and Lawrence E. Cohen. 1990. Structural covariates of homicide rates: Are there any invariances across time and social space? *American Journal of Sociology* 95:922-963.

Langworthy, Robert H. 1988. Community correlates of police agency arrest practices. Paper presented at the annual meeting of the Academy of Criminal Justice Sciences. n.p.

Langworthy, Robert H. and Lawrence F. Travis III. 1997. *Policing in America: A Balance of Forces*. New York, NY: Macmillan Publishing.

Lauritsen, Janet L. 2001. The social ecology of violent victimization: individual and contextual effects in the NCVS. *Journal of Quantitative Criminology* 17:3-32.

Law enforcement officers killed and assaulted, 1986. 1987. Washington, DC: Federal Bureau of Investigation.

Law enforcement officers killed and assaulted, 1987. 1988. Washington, DC: Federal Bureau of Investigation.

Law enforcement officers killed and assaulted, 1988. 1989. Washington, DC: Federal Bureau of Investigation.

Law enforcement officers killed and assaulted, 1989. 1990. Washington, DC: Federal Bureau of Investigation.

Law enforcement officers killed and assaulted, 1990. 1991. Washington, DC: Federal Bureau of Investigation.

Law enforcement officers killed and assaulted, 1991. 1992. Washington, DC: Federal Bureau of Investigation.

Law enforcement officers killed and assaulted, 1992. 1993. Washington, DC: Federal Bureau of Investigation.

Law enforcement officers killed and assaulted, 1993. 1994. Washington, DC: Federal Bureau of Investigation.

Law enforcement officers killed and assaulted, 1994. 1995. Washington, DC: Federal Bureau of Investigation.

Law enforcement officers killed and assaulted, 1995. 1996. Washington, DC: Federal Bureau of Investigation.

Law enforcement officers killed and assaulted, 1996. 1997. Washington, DC: Federal Bureau of Investigation.

Law enforcement officers killed and assaulted, 1997. 1998. Washington, DC: Federal Bureau of Investigation.

Law enforcement officers killed and assaulted, 1998. 1999. Washington, DC: Federal Bureau of Investigation.

Law enforcement officers killed and assaulted, 1999. 2000. Washington, DC: Federal Bureau of Investigation.

Lester, David. 1978a. A study of civilian caused murders of police officers. International *Journal of Criminology and Penology* 6:373-78.

-------. 1978b. Predicting murder rates of police officers in urban areas. *Police Law Quarterly* 7:20-25.

-------. 1980. The murder of police officers: Comparative studies, part I. *Police Studies* 3: 54-57.

-------. 1982. Civilians who kill police officers and police officers who kill civilians: A comparison of American cities. *Journal of Police Science and Administration* 10: 384-87.

Liang, Kyung-Yee and Scott L. Zeger. 1986. Longitudinal data analysis using generalized linear models. *Biometrika* 73:13-22.

Lindgren, Sue A. and Marianne W. Zawitz. 2001. *Linking Uniform Crime Reporting data to other datasets.* Washington, DC: Bureau of Justice Statistics.

Little, Robert E. 1984. Cop-killing: A descriptive analysis of the problem. *Police Studies* 7: 68-76.

Long, Scott J. 1997. *Regression Models for Categorical and Limited Dependent Variables.* Thousand Oaks, CA: Sage Publications.

Lonsway, Kimberly A. 2001. The role of women in community policing: Dismantling the warrior image. Community Links:16-17, September.

Lott, John R. Jr. 2000. Does a helping hand put others at risk? Affirmative action, police departments, and crime. Economic Inquiry 38:239-277.

Lumb, Richard C. and Paul C. Friday. 1997. Impact of pepper spray availability on police officer use of force decisions. *Policing: An International Journal of Police Strategy and Management* 20:173-85.

Lumley, Thomas. 1996. XLISP—stat tools for building generalized estimating equations. Journal of Statistics Software 1:n.p. Available at http://www.jstatsoft.org.

Lynch, James P. 1987. Routine activity and victimization at work. Journal of Quantitative Criminology 3:283-299.

Margarita, Mona C. 1980a. Criminal violence against police. Ph.D. dissertation, State University of New York at Albany. Ann Arbor, MI: University Microfilms International.

Margarita, Mona C. 1980b. Killing the police: Myths and motives. *The Annals* 452:63-71.

Margarita, Mona C. 1980c. Police as victims of violence. *The Justice System Journal* 5:218-233.

Marvell, Thomas B. and Carlisle E. Moody. 1996. Specification problems, police levels, and crime rates. *Criminology* 24:55-72.

Massey, Douglas S. and Nancy A. Denton. 1988. The dimensions of residential segregation. *Social Forces* 67:281-315.

Maxfield, Michael G. 1987. Lifestyle and routine activity theories of crime: Empirical studies of victimization, delinquency, and offender decision-making. *Journal of Quantitative Criminology* 3:275-282.

McDowell, Allen. 2001. Technical support services, College Station, TX:S Stata Corporation, E-mail communication, 15 November.

Menard, Scott. 1991. *Longitudinal Research.* Sage University Paper series on Quantitative Applications in the Social Sciences, 07-076. Thousand Oaks, CA: Sage Publications.

Merton, Robert K. 1938. Social structure and anomie. *American Sociological Review* 3:672-682.

Messner, Steven F. 1982. Poverty, inequality, and the urban homicide rate. *Criminology* 20:103-114.

Messner, Steven F. and Richard Rosenfeld. 1999. Social structure and homicide: theory and research. In Smith, M. Dwayne and Margaret A. Zahn (eds.), *Homicide: A Sourcebook of Social Research.* Thousands Oaks, CA: Sage Publications.

Messner, Steven F. and Kenneth Tardiff. 1986. Economic inequality and levels of homicide: An analysis of urban neighborhoods. *Criminology* 24:297-317.

Micthe, Terance D. and David McDowall. 1993. Contextual effects in models of criminal victimization. *Social Forces* 71:741-759.

Miethe, Terance D., Mark C. Stafford, and J. Scott Long. 1987. Social differentiation in criminal victimization: A test of routine activities/lifestyle theories. *American Sociological Review* 52:184-194.

Miethe, Terance D., Michael Hughes, and David McDowall. 1991. Social change and crime rates: An evaluation of alternative theoretical approaches. *Social Forces* 70:165-185.

Miethe, Terance D. and Robert F. Meier. 1994. Crime and Its Social Context: Toward an Integrated Theory of Offenders, Victims, and Situations. Albany, NY: State University of New York Press.

Morabito, EugeneV. and William G. Doerner. 1997. Police use of less-than-lethal force: Oleoresin capsicum (OC) spray. Policing: An International Journal of Police Strategy and Management 20:680-697.

Morenoff, Jeffrey D., Robert J. Sampson, and Stephen W. Raudenbush. 2001. Neighborhood inequality, collective efficacy, and the spatial dynamic of urban violence. Criminology 39:517-560.

Mulroy, Darrell E. and Julio A. Santiago. 2000. Retro police handguns. Law and Order 48:48-50.

Meyer, C. Kenneth, Brunk, Gregory G., and Laura A. Wilson. 2001. *Sources of Violence in America and Their Consequences for Law Enforcement.* Springfield, IL: Charles C Thomas.

One-officer state police cars raise the risks to cops' lives. 1997. *Law Enforcement News* 28:1,14.

Palmer, Louis J. 1998. *The Death Penalty: An American Citizen's Guide to Understanding Federal and State Laws*. Jefferson, NC: McFarland & Company.

Pampel, Fred C. 2000. *Logistic Regression: A Primer*. Sage University Paper series on Quantitative Applications in the Social Sciences, 07-132. Thousand Oaks, CA: Sage Publications.

Parker, Karen F. 2001. A move toward specificity: Examining urban disadvantage and race-and relationship-specific homicide rates. *Journal of Quantitative Criminology* 17:89-110.

Parker, Karen F. and Patricia L. McCall. 1997. Adding another piece to the inequality-homicide puzzle: The impact of structural inequality on racially disaggregated homicide rates. *Homicide Studies* 1:35-60.

Parker, Karen F. and Patricia L. McCall. 1999. Structural conditions and racial homicide patterns: A look at the multiple disadvantages of areas. *Criminology* 37:447-477.

Parker, Karen F., Patricia L. McCall, and Kenneth C. Land. 1999. Determining social-structural predictors of homicide. In Smith, M. Dwayne and Margaret A. Zahn (eds.), *Homicide: A Sourcebook of Social Research*. Thousands Oaks, CA: Sage Publications.

Peak, Kenneth J. 1993. *Policing in America: Methods, Issues, Challenges*. Upper Saddle River, NJ: Prentice-Hall, Inc.

Pedhazur, Elazar J. 1982. *Multiple Regression in Behavioral Research*. New York, NY: CBS College Publishing.

Pepper spray evaluation project: Results of the introduction of oleoresin capsicum (OC) into the Baltimore County, MD, Police Department. 1995. Final Report submitted to the National Institute of Justice. Alexandria, VA: International Association of Chiefs of Police.

Peterson, Ruth D. and William C. Bailey. 1988. Structural influences on the killing of police: A comparison with general homicides. *Justice Quarterly* 5: 207-233.

[Pinizzotto, Anthony J. and Edward F. Davis]. 1992. *Killed in the line of duty: A study of selected felonious killings of law enforcement officers*. Washington, DC: Federal Bureau of Investigation.

Pinizzotto, Anthony J. and Edward F. Davis. 1997. *In the line of fire: Violence against law enforcement officers.* 1997. Washington, DC: Federal Bureau of Investigation and the National Institute of Justice.

Police use of excessive force: Taking gender into account. 1999. Los Angeles, CA: National Center for Woman in Policing.

Quinet, K. D., D. J. Bordua, and W. Lassiter III. 1997. Line of duty police deaths: A paradoxical trend in felonious homicides in the United States. *Policing and Society* 6:283-296.

Reaves, Brian A. and Pheny Z. Smith. 1995. *Law enforcement management and administrative statistics, 1993: Data for individual state and local agencies with 100 or more officers.* Washington, DC: Bureau of Justice Statistics.

Reaves, Brian A. and Andrew L. Goldberg. 2000. *Local police departments, 1997.* Washington, DC: Bureau of Justice Statistics.

Riksheim, Eric C. and Steven M. Chermak. 1993. Causes of police behavior revisited. *Journal of Criminal Justice* 21:353-382.

Sampson, Robert J. 1985. Neighborhood and crime: The structural determinants of personal victimization. *Journal of Research in Crime and Delinquency* 22:7-40.

-------. 1986. The effects of urbanization and neighborhood characteristics on criminal victimization. In Figlio, Robert M., Simon Hakim, and George F. Rengert (eds.), *Metropolitan Crime Patterns.* Monsey, NY: Criminal Justice Press.

Sampson, Robert J., Jeffrey D. Morenoff, and Felton Earls. 1999. Beyond capital: Spatial dynamics of collective efficacy for children. *American Sociological Review* 64:633-660.

Sampson, Robert J. and John D. Wooldredge. 1987. Linking the micro- and macro-level dimensions of lifestyle-routine activity and opportunity models of predatory victimization. *Journal of Quantitative Criminology* 3:371-393.

Sampson, Robert J. and Stephen W. Raudenbush. 1999. Systematic social observation of public spaces: A new look at disorder in urban neighborhoods. *American Journal of Sociology* 105:603-51.

Sampson, Robert J., Stephen W. Raudenbush, and Felton Earls. 1997. Neighborhoods and violent crime: A multilevel study of collective efficacy. *Science* 277:918-924.

Sampson, Robert J. and W. Byron Groves. 1989. Community structure and crime: testing social-disorganization theory. *American Journal of Sociology* 94:775-802.

Sampson, Robert J. and William Julius Wilson. 1995. Toward a theory of race, crime and urban inequality. In Hagan, John and Ruth D. Peterson (eds.), *Crime and Inequality*. Stanford, CA: Stanford University Press.

Sayrs, Lois W. 1989. *Pooled Time Series Analysis*. Sage University Paper series on Quantitative Applications in the Social Sciences, 07-070. Thousand Oaks, CA: Sage Publications.

Scharf, Peter and Arnold Binder. 1983. *The Badge and the Bullet*. New York, NY: Praeger Books.

Schneider, Victoria W. and Brian Wiersema. 1990. Limits and use of the Uniform Crime Reports. In MacKenzie, Doris Layton, Phyllis Jo Baunach, and Roy R. Roberg (eds.), *Measuring Crime: Large-scale, Long-range Efforts*. Albany, NY: State University of New York Press.

Schendel, J. D., J. L. Shields, and M. S. Katz. 1978. Retention of motor skills: Review. Alexandria, VA: U.S. Army Research Institute for the Behavioral and Social Sciences.

Shaw, Clifford, and Henry McKay. 1969. *Juvenile Delinquency and Urban Areas*, rev. ed. Chicago, IL: University of Chicago Press.

Sherman, Lawrence W. 1980a. Causes of police behavior: The current state of quantitative research. *Journal of Research in Crime and Delinquency* 17:69-100.

-------. 1980b. Perspective on police and violence. *The Annals* 452:1-12.

Sherman, Lawrence W., Patrick R. Gartin, and Michael E. Buerger. 1989. Hot spots of predatory crime: Routine activities and the criminology of place. *Criminology* 27:27-55.

Smith, David M., Bill Robertson, and Peter J. Diggle. 1997. OSWALD: Object-oriented software for the analysis of longitudinal data in S-

PLUS. Available at
http://www.maths.lancs.ac.uk/Software/Oswald/oswald-www/.

Smith, M. Dwayne and Robert Nash Parker. 1980. Type of homicide
and variation in regional rates. *Social Forces* 59:136-147.

Smith, William R., Sharon G. Frazee, and Elizabeth L. Davidson. 2000.
Furthering the integration of routine activity and social
disorganization theories: Small units of analysis and the study of
street robbery as a diffusion process. *Criminology* 38:489-524.

Sorensen, Annemette, Karl E. Taeuber, and Leslie J. Hollingsworth.
1975. Indexes of racial residential segregation for 109 cities in the
United States, 1940 to 1970. *Sociological Focus* 8:125-42.

South, Scott J. and Lawrence E. Cohen. 1985. Unemployment and the
homicide rate: A paradox resolved? *Social Indicators Research*
17:325-43.

Southwick, L. (1998). An economic analysis of murder and accident
risks for police in the United States. *Applied Economics, 30,* 593-
605.

Springer, Stephen M. Community policing: Leading officers into
danger? *FBI Law Enforcement Bulletin* 63:9-12.

StataCorp. 2001. Stata Statistical Software: Release 7.0. College
Station, TX: Stata Corporation.

Strawbridge, Peter and Deirdre Strawbridge. 1990. *A networking guide
to recruitment, selection and probationary training of police
officers in major police departments of the United States of
America.* New York, NY: John Jay College of Criminal Justice.

Thrasher, F. M. 1963. *The Gang: A Study of 1,313 Gangs in Chicago.*
Chicago, IL: University of Chicago Press. (Original work
published in 1927)

Trojanowicz, Robert. 1986. Evaluating a neighborhood foot patrol
program: The Flint, Michigan Project. In Rosenbaum, Dennis
(ed.), *Community Crime Prevention: Does It Work?* Beverly Hills,
CA: Sage Publications.

Turner, Eugene. 1998. *Exploring the U.S. census.* Available at
http://www.csubak.edu/ssric/Modules/CENS/CENSMod/censtoc.h
tm.

U.S. Department of Justice, Bureau of Justice Statistics. 1996a. Law enforcement management and administrative statistics), 1990 [Computer file]. Conducted by U.S. Department of Commerce, Bureau of the Census. ICPSR ed. Ann Arbor, MI: Inter-university Consortium for Political and Social Research [producer and distributor].

-------. 1996b. Law enforcement management and administrative statistics (LEMAS), 1993 [Computer file]. Conducted by U.S. Department of Commerce, Bureau of the Census. ICPSR ed. Ann Arbor, MI: Inter-university Consortium for Political and Social Research [producer and distributor].

-------. 1997. Law enforcement management and administrative statistics, 1987 [Computer file]. Conducted by U.S. Department of Commerce, Bureau of the Census. ICPSR ed. Ann Arbor, MI: Inter-university Consortium for Political and Social Research [producer and distributor].

-------. 1999. Law enforcement management and administrative statistics (LEMAS): 1997 Sample survey of law enforcement agencies [Computer file]. ICPSR version. U.S. Department of Commerce, Bureau of the Census [producer], 1998. Ann Arbor, MI: Inter-university Consortium for Political and Social Research [distributor].

-------. 2000. Law enforcement agency identifiers crosswalk [United States], 1996 [Computer file]. ICPSR ed. Ann Arbor, MI: Inter-university Consortium for Political and Social Research [producer and distributor].

U.S. Department of Justice, Federal Bureau of Investigation. 1999. Uniform Crime Reporting Program data: [United States], 1975-1997 [Police Employee (LEOKA) Data, 1997] [Computer file]. Compiled by the U.S. Department of Justice, Federal Bureau of Investigation. ICPSR ed. Ann Arbor, MI: Inter-university Consortium for Political and Social Research [producer and distributor].

U.S. Department of Justice, Federal Bureau of Investigation. 2000. Uniform Crime Reporting Program data: [United States], 1975-1997 [offenses known and clearances by arrest] [Computer file].

Compiled by the U.S. Department of Justice, Federal Bureau of Investigation. ICPSR ed. Ann Arbor, MI: Inter-university Consortium for Political and Social Research [producer and distributor].

Von Hentig, Hans. 1948. *The Criminal and His Victim.* New Haven, CT: Yale University Press.

Williams, Kirk R. 1984. Economic sources of homicide: Reestimating the effects of poverty and inequality. *American Sociological Review* 49:283-89.

Wilson, James Q. 1975. *Varieties of Police Behavior: The Management of Law and Order in Eight Communities.* New York, NY: Atheneum.

Wilson, James Q. and Barbara Boland. 1978. The effect of the police on crime. *Law and Society Review* 12:367-390.

Wilson, James Q. and Richard J. Hernstein. 1985. *Crime and Human Nature: The Definitive Study of the Causes of Crime.* New York, NY: Simon and Schuster, Inc.

Wilson, Laura A., Brunk, Gregory G., and C. Kenneth Meyer. 1990. Situational Effects in Police Officer Assaults: The Case of Patrol Unit Size. *Police Journal* 63:260-271.

Wilson, William Julius. 1987. The Truly Disadvantaged: The Inner City, the Underclass, and *Public Policy.* Chicago, IL: The University of Chicago Press.

Wolfgang, Marvin E. 1958. *Patterns in Criminal Homicide.* Philadelphia, PA: University of Chicago Press

Wolfgang, Marvin E., and Franco Ferracuti. 1967. *The Subculture of Violence.* Beverly Hills, CA: Sage Publications.

Zeger, Scott L. and Kyung-Yee Liang. 1986. Longitudinal data analysis for discrete and continuous outcomes. *Biometrics* 42:121-130.

Zimring, Franklin. 1972. The medium is the message: Firearm caliber as a determinant of death from assault. *Journal of Legal Studies* *1:97-123.*

Appendix

Table A1: Listing of 190 Jurisdictions Used in the Analysis

1 Abilene, TX	25 Cedar Rapids, IA	49 Eugene, OR	73 Huntsville, AL
2 Akron, OH	26 Charlotte, NC	50 Evansville, IN	74 Independence, MO
3 Albany, NY	27 Chattanooga, TN	51 Flint, MI	75 Indianapolis, IN
4 Albuquerque, NM	28 Chesapeake, VA	52 Fort Lauderdale, FL	76 Inglewood, CA
5 Alexandria, VA	29 Chicago, IL	53 Fort Wayne, IN	77 Irvine, CA
6 Allentown, PA	30 Chula Vista, CA	54 Fort Worth, TX	78 Irving, TX
7 Amarillo, TX	31 Cincinnati, OH	55 Fremont, CA	79 Jackson, MS
8 Anaheim, CA	32 Cleveland, OH	56 Fresno, Ca	80 Jacksonville, FL
9 Anchorage, AK	33 Colorado Springs, CO	57 Fullerton, CA	81 Jersey City, NJ
10 Ann Arbor, MI	34 Columbus, GA	58 Garden Grove, CA	82 Kansas City, KS
11 Arlington, TX	35 Columbus, OH	59 Garland, TX	83 Kansas City, MO
12 Atlanta, GA	36 Concord, CA	60 Gary, IN	84 Knoxville, TN
13 Aurora, CO	37 Corpus Christi, TX	61 Glendale, AZ	85 Lakewood, CO
14 Austin, TX	38 Dallas, TX	62 Glendale, CA	86 Lansing, MI
15 Bakersfield, CA	39 Dayton, OH	63 Grand Rapids, MI	87 Laredo, TX
16 Baltimore, MD	40 Denver, CO	64 Greensboro, NC	88 Lexington, KY
17 Baton Rouge, LA	41 Des Moines, IA	65 Hampton, VA	89 Lincoln, NB
18 Beaumont, TX	42 Detroit, MI	66 Hartford, CT	90 Little Rock, AR
19 Berkeley, CA	43 Durham, NC	67 Hayward, CA	91 Livonia, MI
20 Birmingham, AL	44 El Monte, CA	68 Hialeah, FL	92 Long Beach, CA
21 Boise, ID	45 El Paso, TX	69 Hollywood, FL	93 Los Angeles, CA
22 Boston, MA	46 Elizabeth, NJ	70 Honolulu, HI	94 Louisville, KY
23 Bridgeport, CT	47 Erie, PA	71 Houston, TX	95 Lowell, MA
24 Buffalo, NY	48 Escondido, CA	72 Huntington Beach, CA	96 Lubbock, TX

97 Macon, GA
98 Madison, WI
99 Memphis, TN
100 Mesa, AZ
101 Mesquite, TX
102 Miami, FL
103 Milwaukee, WI
104 Minneapolis, MN
105 Mobile, AL
106 Modesto, CA
107 Montgomery, AL
108 Nashville, TN
109 New Haven, CT
110 New Orleans, LA
111 New York City, NY
112 Newark, NJ
113 Newport News, VA
114 Norfolk, VA
115 Oakland, CA
116 Oceanside, CA
117 Oklahoma City, OK
118 Omaha, NB
119 Ontario, CA
120 Orange, CA
121 Orlando, FL
122 Overland Park, KS

123 Oxnard, CA
124 Pasadena, CA
125 Pasadena, TX
126 Paterson, NJ
127 Peoria, IL
128 Philadelphia, PA
129 Phoenix, AZ
130 Pittsburgh, PA
131 Plano, TX
132 Pomona, CA
133 Portland, OR
134 Portsmouth, VA
135 Providence, RI
136 Raleigh, NC
137 Reno, NV
138 Richmond, VA
139 Riverside, CA
140 Rochester, NY
141 Rockford, IL
142 Sacramento, CA
143 Saint Louis, MO
144 Saint Paul, MN
145 Saint Petersburg, FL
146 Salem, OR
147 Salinas, CA
148 Salt Lake City, UT

149 San Antonio, TX
150 San Bernardino, CA
151 San Diego, CA
152 San Francisco, CA
153 San Jose, CA
154 Santa Ana, CA
155 Santa Rosa, CA
156 Savannah, GA
157 Scottsdale, AZ
158 Seattle, WA
159 Shreveport, LA
160 Simi Valley, CA
161 Sioux Falls, SD
162 South Bend, IN
163 Spokane, WA
164 Springfield, IL
165 Springfield, MA
166 Springfield, MO
167 Stamford, CT
168 Sterling Heights, MI
169 Stockton, CA
170 Sunnyvale, CA
171 Syracuse, NY
172 Tacoma, WA
173 Tallahassee, FL
174 Tampa, FL

175 Tempe, AZ
176 Toledo, OH
177 Topeka, KS
178 Torrance, CA
179 Tucson, AZ
180 Tulsa, OK
181 Vallejo, CA
182 Virginia Beach, VA
183 Waco, TX
184 Warren, MI
185 Washington, DC
186 Waterbury, CT
187 Wichita, KS
188 Winston-Salem, NC
189 Worcester, MA
190 Yonkers, NY

Table A2: Collinearity Diagnostics, 1997

Coefficients

Model	Unstandardized Coefficients		Standardized Coefficient - Beta	t	Sig	Collinearity Statistics	
	B	Std. Error				Tolerance	VIF
1							
(Constant)	-.962	1.312		-.733	.465		
UNIT1_97	-8.665E-04	.003	-.024	-.325	.746	.548	1.826
FOOT97	-2.595E-03	.005	-.034	-.477	.634	.605	1.654
SEMIAUTO97	-.108	.092	-.071	-1.177	.241	.853	1.172
VEST_97	3.500E-02	.077	.027	.452	.652	.891	1.122
CHEM_97	-8.137E-02	.150	-.034	-.541	.589	.778	1.285
FIELD_97	2.832E-04	.000	1.177	3.524	.001	.028	36.091
FEM_97	1.036E-02	.010	.074	1.034	.303	.606	1.651
COLLEGE97	-4.610E-03	.087	-.003	-.053	.958	.839	1.192
ACADEMY97	3.185E-05	.000	.020	.322	.748	.844	1.186
CRIME97	4.381E-06	.000	.283	1.312	.191	.066	15.113
SOUTH	-4.416E-02	.120	-.032	-.367	.714	.399	2.508
POPULATION	-1.243E-06	.000	-1.225	-3.188	.002	.021	47.787
DENSITY	-4.814E-06	.000	-.024	-.270	.788	.395	2.531
FHHKIDS	6.430E-04	.021	.005	.031	.976	.127	7.904
INCOME	1.114E-05	.000	.132	1.099	.273	.215	4.657
GINI	1.490	1.562	.101	.954	.341	.277	3.614
SEGREGATION	-.167	.428	-.043	-.390	.697	.248	4.035
POVERTY	-5.157E-03	.020	-.052	-.253	.800	.074	13.539
UNEMPLOYMENT	1.336E-02	.035	.054	.386	.700	.158	6.347
BLACK	5.364E-03	.005	.146	1.086	.279	.171	5.856
RSTABILITY	3.617E-03	.010	.040	.362	.718	.252	3.965
MALES1529	-1.438E-02	.029	-.045	-.492	.623	.368	2.717
DIVORCE	1.759E-02	.030	.057	.582	.562	.324	3.089
ARRESTS97	2.659E-05	.000	.354	1.429	.155	.050	19.822

Collinearity Diagnostics

Model	Dimension	Eigenvalue	Condition Index	Variance Proportion (Constant)
1	1	17.829	1.000	.00
	2	2.765	2.539	.00
	3	.904	4.442	.00
	4	.895	4.463	.00
	5	.631	5.317	.00
	6	.485	6.063	.00
	7	.409	6.600	.00
	8	.251	8.425	.00
	9	.164	10.439	.00
	10	.134	11.545	.00
	11	.119	12.241	.00
	12	9.046E-02	14.039	.00
	13	6.867E-02	16.112	.00
	14	5.787E-02	17.552	.00
	15	4.802E-02	19.268	.00
	16	3.922E-02	21.321	.00
	17	2.786E-02	25.298	.00
	18	2.481E-02	26.804	.00
	19	1.606E-02	33.317	.00
	20	1.195E-02	38.632	.00
	21	1.013E-02	41.947	.00
	22	9.351E-03	43.664	.00
	23	6.904E-03	50.817	.00
	24	2.743E-03	80.614	.01
	25	6.096E-04	171.016	.99

Table A3: Principal Components Analysis

KMO and Bartlett's Test

Kaiser-Meyer-Olkin Measure of Sampling Adequacy		.741
Bartlett's Test of Sphericity	Approx. Chi-Square	1573.268
	df	55
	Sig.	.000

Communalities

	Initial	Extraction
DENSITY	1.000	.745
FHHKIDS	1.000	.799
INCOME	1.000	.744
GINI	1.000	.579
SEGREGATION	1.000	.631
POVERTY	1.000	.878
UNEMPLOYMENT	1.000	.702
BLACK	1.000	.650
RSTABILITY	1.000	.866
MALE1529	1.000	.875
DIVORCE	1.000	.678

Extraction Method: Principal Component Analysis.

Total Variance Explained

Component	Initial Eigenvalues			Extraction Sums of Squared Loadings			Rotation Sums of Squared Loadings		
	Total	% of Variance	Cumulative %	Total	% of Variance	Cumulative %	Total	% of Variance	Cumulative %
1	5.348	48.616	48.616	5.348	48.616	48.616	5.041	45.830	45.830
2	1.452	13.196	61.812	1.452	13.196	61.812	1.678	15.259	61.089
3	1.347	12.249	74.061	1.347	12.249	74.061	1.427	12.972	74.061
4	.832	7.560	81.621						
5	.625	5.685	87.306						
6	.560	5.091	92.396						
7	.317	2.882	95.278						
8	.191	1.733	97.011						
9	.144	1.310	98.321						
10	.125	1.136	99.457						
11	5.978E-02	.543	100.000						

Extraction Method: Principal Component Analysis.

continued

Table A3 (continued): Principal Components Analysis

Unrotated Component Matrix[a]

	Component		
	1	2	3
POVERTY	.891	.286	4.192E-02
FHHKD	.885	.119	4.849E-02
INCOME	-.815	-.173	.223
BLACK	.804	-3.976E-02	-4.209E-02
UNEMPLOYMENT	.792	5.645E-02	.267
SEGREGATION	.773	-.181	-1.885E-02
GINI	.726	.173	-.151
DIVORCE	.599	-7.551E-02	-.560
MALE1529	-.161	.904	.178
RSTABILITY	.518	-.649	.420
DENSITY	.236	.118	.822

Extraction Method: Principal Component Analysis.
a. 3 components extracted.

Rotated Component Matrix[a]

	Component		
	1	2	3
POVERTY	.914	-5.842E-02	-5.842E-02
FHHKD	.869	.102	.102
INCOME	-.858	-1.342E-02	-1.342E-02
BLACK	.770	.230	.230
GINI	.760	-2.492E-03	-2.492E-03
UNEMPLOYMENT	.730	.155	.155
SEGREGATION	.704	.360	.360
DIVORCE	.648	.179	.179
MALE1529	2.250E-02	-.901	-.901
RSTABILITY	.281	.783	.783
DENSITY	.121	8.276E-04	8.276E-04

Extraction Method: Principal Component Analysis.
Rotation Method: Varimax with Kaiser Normalization.
a. Rotation converged in 4 iterations.

Component Transformation Matrix

Component	1	2	3
1	.960	.242	.140
2	.228	-.968	.106
3	-.161	.070	.984

Extraction Method: Principal Component Analysis.
Rotation Method: Varimax with Kaiser Normalization

Figure A1: Hat Diagonals After Removal Of Influential Cases

A. 1997

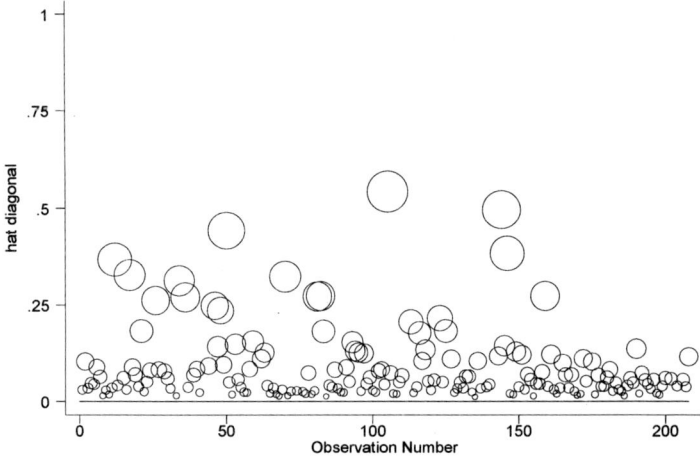

B. 1993

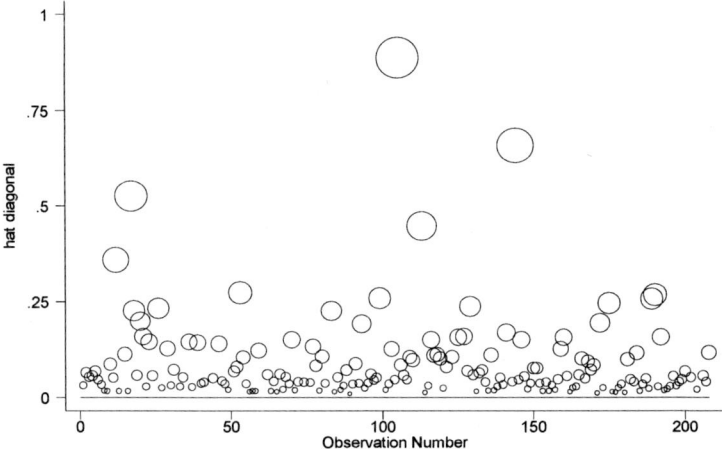

Figure A1 (continued)

C. 1990

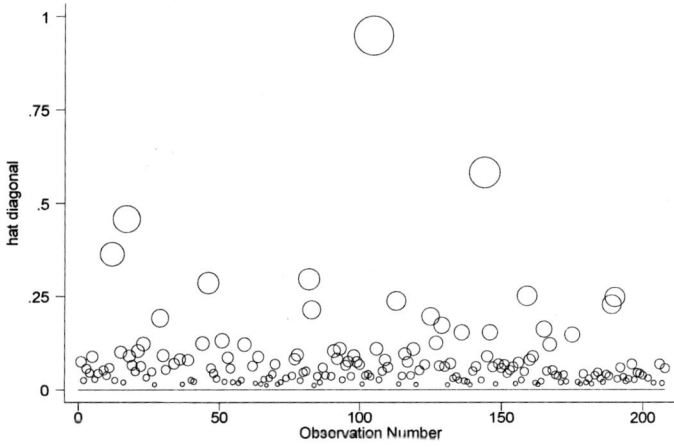

D. 1987

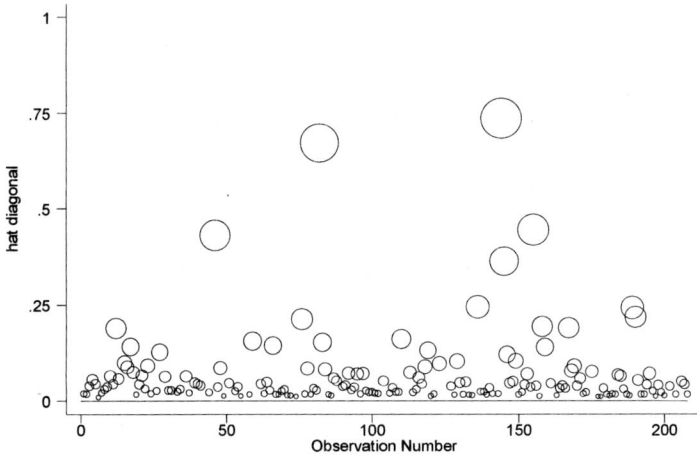

Figure A2: Deviance Residuals for Trimmed Model with Interaction Term

A. 1997

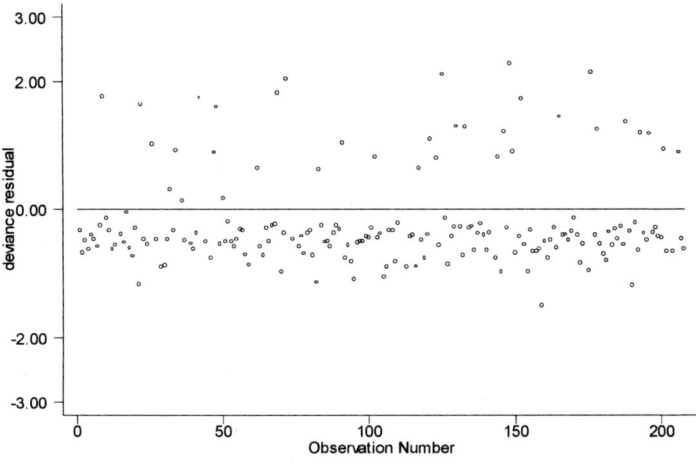

B. 1993

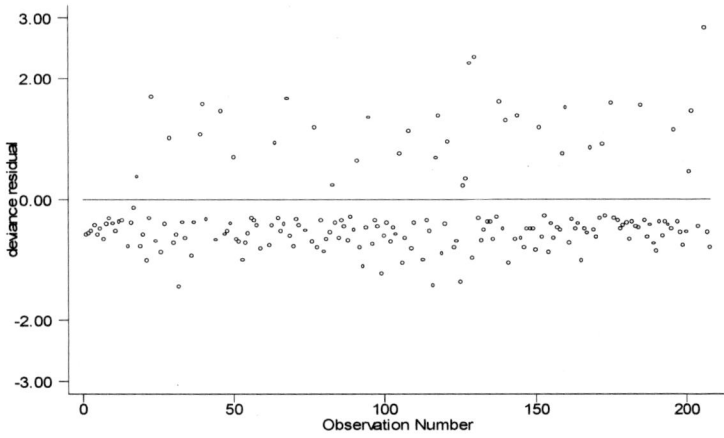

Figure A2 (continued)

C. 1990

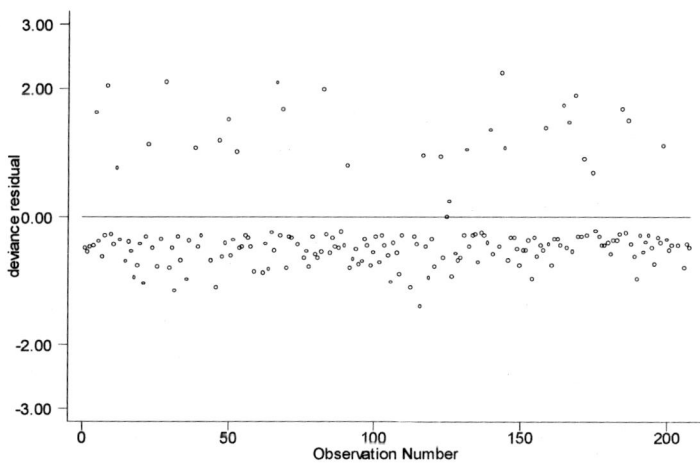

D. 1987

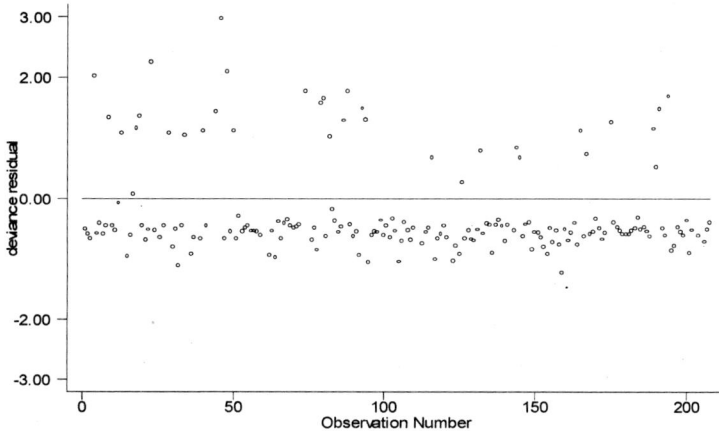

Table A4: Comparing GEE Poisson and GEE Negative Binomial Estimates

Variable	A. GEE Poisson			B. GEE Negative Binomial		
	IRR (e^β)	Std. Err.	P>|z|	IRR (e^β)	Std. Err.	P>|z|
DEPRIVATION	1.32946	0.12480	0.002	1.29304	0.11756	0.005
DENSITY	1.08731	0.14444	0.529	1.09219	0.14402	0.504
STABILITY	1.19451	0.11949	0.076	1.18755	0.11666	0.080
FIELD2	1.01794	0.00791	0.022	1.01919	0.00859	0.024
ARRESTS	1.00006	7.98e-06	0.000	1.00007	8.90e-06	0.000
ARRESTS*DENSITY	0.99999	1.99e-06	0.000	.999991	2.23e-06	0.000
FEMALE	1.03375	0.01740	0.049	1.03380	0.01775	0.053
SOUTH	1.53383	0.34026	0.054	1.54237	0.33828	0.048
Constant	-2.77426	0.20991	0.000	-2.85735	0.210310	0.000
Wald χ^2	466.21, $p \leq$ .0000			405.93, $p \leq$ .0000		

Notes: N obvs. = 756; Scale parameters (α) = 1 and .1712 for Poisson and negative binomial regressions, respectively; correlation = AR(1); Std. Err. = robust standard errors; constants are not exponentiated. Poisson goodness-of-fit test from pooled estimator = 499.49, p = 1.0000.

Table A5: SEMIAUTO Suspicious Values and Corrections (N = 15)

Case ID/City Name	'87	'90	'93	'97	Correction
25 Cedar Rapids	0	0	1	0	'97 = 1
36 Concord	1	0	1	1	'90 = 1
43 Durham	0	0	1	0	'97 = 1
53 Fort Wayne	0	0	1	0	'97 = 1
56 Fresno	1	0	1	1	'90 = 1
64 Greensboro	1	0	1	1	'90 = 1
87 Laredo	0	0	1	0	'97 = 1
10 Mesquite	0	0	1	0	'97 = 1
127 Peoria	0	0	1	0	'97 = 1
130 Pittsburgh	0	0	1	0	'97 = 1
142 Sacramento	1	0	1	1	'90 = 1
145 St. Petersburg	0	1	0	0	'93 & '97 = 1
154 Santa Ana	0	0	1	0	'97 = 1
170 Sunnyvale	1	0	1	1	'90 = 1
177 Topeka	0	1	0	1	'93 = 1

Table A6: OC Suspicious Values and Corrections (N = 41)

Case ID / City Name	'90	'93	'97	Correction
2 Akron	1	0	1	'93 = 1
6 Allentown	0	1	0	'97 = 1
15 Bakersfield	1	0	1	'93 = 1
18 Beaumont	1	0	1	'93 = 1
22 Boston	1	0	1	'93 = 1
24 Buffalo	1	0	0	'93 & '97 = 1
25 Cedar Rapids	1	0	1	'93 = 1
28 Chesapeake	1	0	1	'93 = 1
31 Cincinnati	1	0	0	'93 & '97 = 1
34 Columbus (GA)	1	0	0	'93 & '97 = 1
38 Dallas	0	1	0	'97 = 1
42 Detroit	1	0	1	'93 = 1
45 El Paso	1	0	0	'93 & '97 = 1
51 Flint	1	0	1	'93 = 1
55 Fremont	1	0	1	'93 = 1
56 Fresno	1	0	1	'93 = 1
60 Gary	1	0	1	'93 = 1
67 Hayward	1	0	1	'93 = 1
68 Hialeah	1	0	1	'93 = 1
69 Hollywood	1	1	0	'97 = 1
73 Huntsville	1	0	1	'93 = 1
79 Jackson	1	0	1	'93 = 1
81 Jersey City	0	1	0	'97 = 1
82 Kansas City (KS)	1	0	1	'93 = 1
85 Lakewood	1	1	0	'97 = 1
86 Lansing	1	0	1	'93 = 1

Table A6 (continued): OC Suspicious Values and Corrections

Case ID/City Name	'90	'93	'97	Correction
99 Memphis	1	1	0	'97 = 1
101 Mesquite	1	0	1	'93 = 1
102 Miami	1	0	0	'93 & '97 = 1
108 Nashville	1	0	0	'93 & '97 = 1
115 Oakland	1	0	1	'93 = 1
116 Oceanside	1	0	1	'93 = 1
119 Ontario	1	0	1	'93 = 1
121 Orlando	1	0	1	'93 = 1
128 Philadelphia	1	0	1	'93 = 1
142 Sacramento	1	0	1	'93 = 1
145 St. Petersburg	1	0	1	'93 = 1
149 San Antonio	1	1	0	'97 = 1
165 Springfield (MA)	1	0	1	'93 = 1
170 Sunnyvale	1	0	1	'93 = 1
171 Syracuse	1	0	1	'93 = 1

Table A7: VEST Suspicious Values and Corrections (N = 24)

Case ID/City Name	'90	'93	'97	Correction
1 Abilene	1	0	1	'93 = 1
6 Allentown	0	1	0	'97 = 1
8 Anaheim	1	0	0	93 & 97 = 1
20 Birmingham	0	1	0	'97 = 1
21 Boise	1	0	0	93 & 97 = 1
24 Buffalo	0	1	0	'97 = 1
28 Chesapeake	0	1	0	'97 = 1
35 Columbus (OH)	0	1	0	'97 = 1
41 Des Moines	1	0	1	'93 = 1
57 Fullerton	0	1	0	'97 = 1
61 Glendale (AZ)	0	1	0	'97 = 1
68 Hialeah	0	1	0	'97 = 1
70 Honolulu	1	0	0	93 & 97 = 1
77 Irvine	1	0	1	'93 = 1
97 Macon	0	1	0	'97 = 1
103 Milwaukee	1	1	0	'97 = 1
109 New Haven	1	1	0	'97 = 1
123 Oxnard	1	1	0	'97 = 1
140 Rochester	1	0	1	'93 = 1
148 Salt Lake City	0	1	0	'97 = 1
150 San Bernardino	1	0	1	'93 = 1
160 Simi Valley	1	0	0	93 & 97 = 1
166 Springfield (MO)	0	1	0	'97 = 1
167 Stamford	1	1	0	'97 = 1

Table A8: COLLEGE Suspicious Values and Corrections (N = 11)

Case ID/City Name	'87	'90	'93	'97	Correction
54 Fort Worth	0	1	0	0	'93 & '97 = 1
56 Fresno	0	0	1	0	'97 = 1
79 Jackson	1	0	0	1	'90 & '93 = 1
133 Portland	1	0	0	1	'90 & '93 = 1
149 San Antonio	0	1	0	0	'93 & '97 = 1
156 Savannah	0	0	1	0	'97 = 1
159 Shreveport	0	0	1	0	'97 = 1
163 Spokane	1	1	1	0	'97 = 1
168 Sterling Hts.	1	1	1	0	'97 = 1
176 Toledo	0	1	1	0	'97 = 1

Index